P9-DFT-595

how **to** start a home-based

Event Planning Business

HOME-BASED BUSINESS SERIES

how **to** start a home-based

Event Planning Business

Second Edition

Jill S. Moran, CSEP

The Globe Pequot Press

GUILFORD, CONNECTICUT

This book's purpose is to provide accurate and authoritative information on the topics covered. It is sold with the understanding that neither the author nor the publisher is engaged in rendering legal, financial, accounting, or other professional services. Neither The Globe Pequot Press nor the author assumes any liability resulting from action taken based on the information included herein. Mention of a company name does not constitute endorsement.

To buy books in quantity for corporate use or incentives, call **(800) 962–0973** or e-mail **premiums@GlobePequot.com.**

Copyright © 2004, 2007 Morris Book Publishing, LLC

All rights reserved. No part of this book may be reproduced or transmitted in any form by any means, electronic or mechanical, including photocopying and recording, or by any information storage and retrieval system, except as may be expressly permitted by the 1976 Copyright Act or by the publisher. Requests for permission should be made in writing to The Globe Pequot Press, P.O. Box 480, Guilford, Connecticut 06437.

Text design: Nancy Freeborn

ISSN: 1548-1565
ISBN: 978-0-7627-4399-5

Manufactured in the United States of America
Second Edition/First Printing

This book is dedicated to my family.

Acknowledgments

I would like to acknowledge the following:

Jill Epstein and Sue Krawitz for their research material on the variety of professional designations and educational resources available for study in the area of events, hospitality, meetings, tourism, and conference management.

The University of Nevada, Las Vegas, for its resource information on educational institutions and programs with an events focus.

The International Special Events Society for setting professional industry standards and for offering the Certified Special Events designation and study program.

I would also like to thank my family, clients, colleagues, and friends for their support and inspiration in writing this book.

My father, Russell Schofield, who supported me in everything I did and taught me to believe that I could be whatever I chose to be. My mother, Amelia, who planted the first creative seed in me and continues to feed it with projects, inspiration, and example. My sister, Jane, and brothers, Billie and Brady, who shared their gifts with me throughout my life, helping me build and refine my business.

My husband, Peter, for his willingness to walk down the road of life alongside me. My children, Kate, Kevin, and Paige, for their understanding, support, confidence, and patience with their crazy event planning mom!

My clients, who trust me with their projects and defer to me for my creative and professional advice, many of whom have become dear friends and forever left a mark on my life.

My event colleagues, who share their ideas, seek my advice, believe in my leadership, and support me with their talents and energy.

My close friends, who listen, advise, and laugh with me as I negotiate the many twists and turns of my life.

For all of these wonderful people that I have been blessed to have in my life, I am grateful. All have added to my confidence to plan event after event and put it all down in writing for others to learn from.

Contents

So You Want to Get Serious about Planning Special Events?

Maybe you always knew you were meant to be a special event planner. You know who you are! You're the one who organizes the class dances, the family reunions, the friends' birthday parties, and the school fund-raisers. You get the call to run the school auction, "fun day," or town road race. You decide to organize a float in the town parade just because. If any of these scenarios sounds familiar, you've identified your slot in life and can begin to take the first step in realizing a life-long dream! Maybe you never thought making a living could be so much fun. Or you weren't willing to put the time and energy into for-malizing your business. Whatever the case, the following pages will help you to identify your skill set, zero in on the gaps, give you sugges-tions on filling them, and set up an event planning business in your home.

Whether your goal is to be better equipped to head up the school fund-raisers or to launch a full-scale wedding planning business, you'll get a broad perspective on how to better prepare yourself for the fun but challenging business of planning special events.

Self-Assessment

So how do you know if event planning is right for you? Take this quick quiz:

- What would you rather do . . . watch a play or be in one?
- On a rainy Saturday . . . read a book or redecorate your living room?
- Drive or be driven?
- Plan the menu for the holidays or let your sister bring the food?
- Host a party or attend one?

- Do masquerade parties excite or frustrate you?
- Are your favorite shops fabric boutiques, design centers, and art supply stores?
- Can you juggle several tasks at once? Or several projects at once?
- Do you enjoy solving problems?
- Do you love spontaneity . . . or hate it?

Your responses should tell you if you're someone who likes to be actively involved in the things you do and tends toward creative activities—or if you'd be overwhelmed by the dynamic process of overseeing an event.

If you like the excitement of taking the ordinary and turning it into the extraordinary, the good news is that you hold one of the basic traits critical to being a good event planner. The bad news, however, is that you can't operate a business on flair alone. You must add organization, good business sense, and continual professional training to the mix to build a successful event planning business.

If this makes you a bit nervous, fear not. The following pages will show you how to combine your strengths with the right support systems to realize your dream of becoming an event planner.

The Ingredients of a Successful Event Planner

So what makes a good event planner? Here are some terms you might use to describe one:

- High energy
- Organized
- Creative
- Self-motivated
- Multitasker
- Driven

- Good with people
- Extroverted
- Calm
- Can-do attitude
- Attentive to detail
- Motivator
- Entrepreneur
- Leader
- Listener
- Focused
- Cooperative
- Flexible
- Passionate
- Team player

As you can see, it takes a lot of flexibility and sometimes a "Jekyll-and-Hyde" personality to handle all the details of the event process. In the initial stages of planning an event, you have to be a salesperson—persistent, knowledgeable, and persuasive—when writing your proposal and convincing the prospect to give you the job. In pulling together the elements of the event, you must be creative, thorough, and open to ideas from vendors. You must be comfortable asserting yourself but also be flexible enough to take advice from the professionals you'll hire to help produce your event. As you draft and present contracts, your business hat must be firmly set atop your head. You'll need to cover all the details in writing, outlining your responsibilities to vendors and to clients. When creating timelines, you must think through all the details that will take place from the moment the client says, "You're hired!" to the final "Great job!" When requesting pay-

Professional Assessment

I Have . . .	I Need . . .	I Must . . .
An understanding of how to price events, but little skill at keeping track of expenses	Control of my finances	Hire a part-time accountant or bookkeeper
Ideas on how to make spaces into fabulous events; the ability to create themes that are new and exciting; a sense for what my company is all about, but no skill at putting it in writing	A good writer and graphic designer	Partner with a marketing company, printer, or intern from a local college who can create brochures and work on proposals
The desire to plan event after event	A way to get business— a marketing plan	Network, join civic or professional groups, and follow up on sales leads
Lots of good ideas	The skills to pull everything together	Hire good vendors—prop houses, designers, and builders who can bring my ideas to life

ment and keeping track of expenses, you must be organized and detailed, keeping your client up to date on any changes or additional costs during the planning process.

Clearly, it takes a lot of different characteristics to become accomplished at owning your own business—and being successful at it. You may have some natural talent for parts of the process but cringe at the thought of other tasks. My advice is to learn to set your limits and get the support you need to balance what you have with what you need. Even if you don't see yourself as a master juggler, learn to hire a few extra arms to help you keep the balls in the air.

More Self-Assessment:
What Do You Have? What Do You Need?

You love to have flowers around but couldn't arrange them if your life depended on it . . . you know the colors you want but have no clue how to get all the blooms to stand up and look good. So what do you do? Hook up with a florist who will work with you to bring your ideas to life.

The same concept holds true for the business

responsibilities you'll have as an event planner—not to mention administration, coordination, marketing, and risk management skills necessary to successfully execute each event. Use the skills you have; develop or source out the skills you need.

On some projects, I handle the decor, props, and linens. I pull the designs together, even purchase specialty fabric and make the sheer overlays with hand-sewn tassels on each corner. This takes time to purchase, produce, and set up. If the budget and time frame allow me to do it, great! But realistically, it depends what other projects are going on and if it's feasible for me to handle all the internal details to complete the look of the event. On other projects I hire a linen company to ship the linens, and perhaps even to set them up for me. I enjoy the full start-to-finish side of planning sometimes, yes, but it isn't always efficient for me to operate that way. It takes me away from selling or managing, which is equally important—if not more so—in growing and maintaining my business. This is where building a full vendor support network is critical. Sometimes, even if you have the skills, it may be more cost and time effective to source out tasks to others, so you can focus on the management piece of your business.

Laying the Foundation: Skills

Take stock of your present skill set. What qualities and skills do you possess that will help you provide event planning services? Do you come from a hospitality background, for instance? Do you have experience in marketing, communications, or entertainment? You probably have skills you've developed from previous jobs, and it's time now to take a serious look at transitioning those talents into the event planning arena. Once you have assessed your strengths and made the commitment to start your business, there are many opportunities to round out your skill set to offer the services of a full-service event planning company.

Event Skills

Talk to the pros. Contact area planners, or meet with facilities that use planners and see what they look for. Become an apprentice or understudy with an event planning company. Start at the lowest level possible to fully understand what goes into the overall process. Work through all the levels of activities, from setup to sales to breakdown. If you feel you have a general understanding of the business from a prior job or position but need to dive into the details, attend industry meetings that offer educational seminars to focus on the specifics. Read up on the latest trends. Take a class. Wendy Joblon, of Wendy Joblon Special Event Planner, left her position at a country club to open her own event planning business. She had worked on outings and weddings at the club for many years and had a complete knowledge of the planning process before she started out on her own.

When I decided to become certified as an event planner, I signed up for a three-week course on fund-raising events to gain a better perspective from a specialist in this area and round out my understanding of these events. I met many interesting people and learned some new tricks on how to present budgets to nonprofit boards of directors. The mind-set you need to produce these events is the polar opposite of what corporate clients call for, and the course was a real eye-opener for me. This was a class offered in my community through the Boston Learning Center, an adult education program that offers educational opportunities in many towns surrounding the city. It was not related to a degree program or university, but it provided excellent insight delivered by a seasoned event professional. More and more degree programs are popping up, too, so investigate these options as well. Check your newspaper, high school flyers, or community college calendars for sessions related to the event or meeting industry. There may be more training right in your backyard than you're aware of! (I'll tell you more about educational programs for planners, as well as the certification process, in chapter 13 and the appendices.)

Besides entering a degree program, signing up for continuing education, or getting on-the-job training, you could find a mentor who is willing to share his or her know-how with you. A colleague who specializes in social events gave me numerous tips and contact names for a wedding I was planning. The planning process was similar to that for the corporate events I'd produced, but my friend pointed out a few of the nuances that characterize a successful wedding. I just didn't have wedding cakes or a justice of the peace filed away in my contacts folder! As long as you won't be direct competition, most seasoned professionals are willing to share some pearls of wisdom with a fledgling.

Other critical components of your start-up include business skills, management skills, selling skills, and technical skills. While you can certainly hire specialists to fill such needs, when you're just starting out you may not have the willingness (or ability) to spend money in these areas. Check out some current books on time management, business planning, budgeting, and managing a staff from your local library. Many of these topics are covered in the best-seller list by authors boasting fresh ideas on the subject. Be willing and ready to change your approach so your business can get off to the right start. Take classes at your local high school on general business topics. Many business software programs also come with material that can help you familiarize yourself with the process of running a company.

Business Skills

Managing a business is no easy task. There are daily activities you must do to keep things running smoothly. First and foremost is keeping track of your expenses and income—the latter being one of the main reasons you're going into business. A good software program such as Quick-Books by Intuit will allow you to invoice your clients, write checks, keep track of account details, and prepare for tax time. You can order personalized business checks through Intuit, which help in presenting your company in a professional manner. The program even allows you to personalize your invoices and track multiple jobs from one client. I've found that the best way to become versed with any new software is simply to use it. Even a basic spreadsheet program such as

Microsoft Excel will allow you to keep track of itemized expenses and will help you price your events properly. Start using these business programs at the beginning, and you'll soon be proficient and efficient at budgeting, forecasting, and controlling the finances of your company.

Management Skills

Managing the people you come in contact with in the event process can be an equally challenging prospect. In the event world you'll be dealing with your client, the setup crew, the chef, the servers, the photographer, the entertainer, and even the guests. You must be able to listen, assuage, persuade, consult, support, convince, and inspire—sometimes all in the same fifteen-minute period! It's a good idea to be aware of your own natural talents in this area, and to find ways to improve upon them. While it's easy to hire support on the technical side or even on the selling side, ultimately *you* are the one who inspires, supervises, motivates, and manages your company and those who work for you.

If you feel you are challenged in the people department, get some training. Take an honest look at how people respond to you when they're working for you. Watch how you deliver your requests. Do you show appreciation for a job well done? Can you criticize constructively? Can you fire and hire people? Can you bring your creative energies and forces out in a positive and complete way . . . getting your point across and giving the event team the information they need to make it happen? All these things are done in the course of running an event business and are skills that can make the difference between good and great!

I read business magazines such as *Inc.* and *Fortune* and check out new business books from the library for inspiration and fresh ideas. Even taking a course or a seminar can help you strengthen your skills and keep your techniques contemporary and fresh. The local chamber of commerce or professional business groups will list these in the newspaper on an ongoing basis. The best way to stay on top of your management style is to ask for feedback, listen to the responses, and take action. Be honest and critical of yourself and your events, and you'll always be working toward improving upon what you've created.

Selling Skills

As a company owner *you* are the best advertisement for your business. Present yourself with confidence. Exemplify the quality and style your company offers. Gather great success stories to share. Sell your company to your colleagues, friends, business associates, and potential clients. If you don't enjoy talking to people—on the phone or in person—to ask for business, you can certainly hire someone to do it for you. Be prepared to pay for the service either through a commission (the most motivating) or for a flat fee. You will need to monitor the success of your sales representative to ensure that you're getting your money's worth.

My greatest challenge is to be selling and producing at the same time, in order to keep business in the pipeline and create a continuous flow of income. This is crucial to the financial strength and viability of your company as a full-service, full-time enterprise. Much depends on the economy and the seasonal nature of some areas of the event business, of course. Still, it's a great goal to set!

Technical Skills

Can you operate your computer with relative ease? Can you work through creating and delivering a PowerPoint presentation? Can you design a flowchart and seating chart for an event? Can you set up a spreadsheet with complete costs in order to create a budget? If not, start practicing! I've found that most of my computer knowledge has come from simply using my computer again and again. You may want to grab a *Microsoft Office for Dummies* book or take a refresher course on using a basic office computer program. You will need to be versed in some basic office programs to present and track your events in a professional way. Most of it will just take time and constant practice.

Still, while I've learned the basic programs through hours of use, when a real computer glitch hits I call "The Computer Guy"—an independent repair technician who comes to my home, usually the same day, to get me up and running again. He suggests updates or new products that will enhance my system and even orders and installs them for me. This is an area that I definitely need help in, and it has been invaluable having the right person to come to my rescue!

Finding Your Niche:
Types of Event Planning Services

What do you enjoy? What are you good at? These questions can help you pinpoint the area you could most successfully deliver event services in. Then you can expand as your confidence and skills grow.

What follows are some general descriptions of the various types of planning you might focus on. (Each will be dealt with in depth in a later chapter.) What interests you or intrigues you? Could you develop the team you need to pull off these events?

Social Events

If you enjoy creating events that celebrate life milestones, the social client is for you. These are weddings, birthdays, bar and bat mitzvahs, anniversary events, and the like. They are usually onetime affairs, but the possibility of follow-up business exists if you focus on creating a good relationship and ensure that the event is produced in a high-quality way. These clients can and will refer you to friends or relatives—or even call back themselves when the next family celebration takes place.

A social client can be fairly emotional. You'll see social clients joyous over their special celebrations, overwhelmed by the prospect of making choices, and shocked at the budget that goes into creating the event of their dreams. It takes patience, support, and persuasion to bring together the "wish" list with the "can-get" list. At times you must wait out a client's emotional moments while remaining grounded enough to carry off the event without a hitch! At many social events, too, you'll have several contacts or layers of decision makers to deal with. Finding out who is the ultimate decision maker will be important, but always remember to give credence to the wishes of all parties. A bride may be sketching out her plans, for instance, only to be stifled by a mother or father who really wants to invite the entire country club instead of the sorority. Being able to balance these two goals for the same event can be challenging! The theme of the bar mitzvah will have to appeal to the younger set attending but also not create an uncomfortable or inappropriate setting for the adult attendees. These kinds of balancing acts are where the true value of a planner comes into play!

Corporate Events

The corporate market offers a very different feel from the social. While some of the same characteristics are present—a long chain of command, committees with different ideas to be addressed, budgetary restraints—the corporate client is approached differently. Most companies are used to hiring professionals to fulfill certain specialized roles and will often let the planner make final recommendations and suggestions. Corporate clients are less emotionally volatile than social clients, but their expectations for creativity, quality, and execution are every bit as high.

A single corporate client may have multiple programs that you can provide for, in departments such as sales, human resources, and marketing. Creating a lasting relationship is thus

critical with the corporate client—it can give you additional business beyond the first event. Networking internally will be necessary, because the sales department might not know what HR is doing, and vice versa. From company outings to award dinners, team-building events to trade show events, depending on your interest and capabilities, a corporate client can give you a smorgasbord of event opportunities.

Downsides to the corporate market include the changing economy and changes in management. Companies have high seasons when money is flowing and they're comfortable spending on either marketing or internal events. Then come the seasons of cutbacks, and the extras like company outings and luxurious client events are eliminated. In addition, you may form a strong relationship with a top decision maker at one of your best companies—then see him or her change jobs. If other executives with their own favorite event planner take over, you may lose your ongoing relationship. Still, if your original contact moves to a competing company, you could gain a new client—so stay in touch!

Regional Events

If you want to focus on one area and become the "go-to" person there, think about becoming a destination planner. A "DMC"—destination management company—provides hospitality services or event-related services in a specific geographic location. Activities can include meeting out-of-town guests at airports and transferring them to a hotel, group activities for visitors attending a conference, or team-building events and other

Event Categories

- Social events
- Children's events
- Weddings
- Corporate events
- Outings
- Fairs and festivals
- Parades
- Birthday parties
- Bar and bat mitzvahs
- Religious events
- Fund-raising events
- Awards dinners
- Sales events
- Incentive events
- College events
- Event marketing
- Hospitality events
- Tours and charters
- Destination management
- Meeting planning
- Team building
- Product launches
- Ground-breaking events
- Business celebrations

Event Services

- Invitations
- Entertainment
- Talent agency
- Decor
- Florals
- Rentals
- Linens
- Incentive gifts
- Photography
- Videography
- Inflatables
- Novelty items
- DJ
- Staffing
- Tent scenery and backdrops
- Audiovisual/sound
- Lighting production
- Catering
- Carnival and casino rentals
- Transportation
- Parking
- Security
- Ice sculptures
- Bakery/wedding cakes

- Bleachers/skyboxes
- Amusements/games
- Professional speakers
- Novelties/caricatures
- Costumes
- Decorative and specialty fabrics
- Flags/banners
- Ticketing services
- Restroom trailers
- Insurance
- Special effects/ pyrotechnics
- Calligraphy

general corporate or social events held in the area. Other programs associated with local conventions or conferences include themed events, recreational or "spouse" programs, "step-on" tours (which familiarize visitors with highlights of the area), museum tours, and hotel arrangements. For success in this area, familiarity with local tourist attractions, special venues, and restaurants is a must. It's also important to have great resource people to support you during busy times. You'll need to establish relationships with hotels, restaurants, convention and visitor bureaus, and the chamber of commerce to get leads on groups coming into town well in advance.

Fairs and Festivals

Fairs and festivals take place in every town and city, every year. These events are held to celebrate holidays or town anniversaries, to host sporting events, or as fund-raisers. They involve large numbers of people, from volunteers to attendees to vendors. A good planner is needed to manage the process from setup to teardown. If you like to work big, these events are for you! You must have a great sense of organization, logistics, and contingency planning. Ultimate people skills are crucial here, because you often have to deal with permits, town officials, and the press. The vendor lists for fairs and festivals include tenting companies, staging companies, and lighting and power supply vendors; often they also involve artists, crafters, and the selling of stalls or booths. Crowd management and safety are focal points, as are advertising, sponsorship, and public relations. A good sense of the area and the attendee interests is a must if the fair is to draw both vendors and visitors.

Children's Events

If you enjoy children and have a tolerance for noise, children's events can be the niche for you! Birthdays, bar and bat mitzvahs, and annual school events can offer an opportunity to bring laughter and magic into the lives of children and take a huge burden of stress off parents who don't know where to go for the clown, singing storyteller, balloon artist, or reptile show. If you gather a wealth of resources for this market, you can provide new and exciting themes and entertainment for young folks. Advertise yourself as offering the newest and most unusual theme parties for the small set. Extend your services to offer crafts, invitations, party favors, and the like. With more families having both Mom and Dad working full time, time can be a valuable commodity; pulling together special events often just doesn't fit into the schedule. Price your services right, and your referrals can keep your business going strong.

Fund-Raisers

Many fund-raising events are driven by committees of volunteers who are passionate about their cause. Events are held every week to raise money for schools, hospitals, and associations or for special causes or people in need. While the many volunteers who rally behind the cause make up the engine that drives an event's success, a good navigator behind the steering wheel is essential. As a chairperson of a fund-raising event, you'd be responsible for various committees such as sponsorship, decorating, silent auction, and communications. Knowledge of the overall process and keen interpersonal skills to manage the volunteers are critical to the success of a fund-raising planner. The ability to garner support from corporate sponsors or local vendors and be a spokesperson for the cause is equally vital. While a board of influential advisers can drive attendance and large donations, an understanding of the market and community is helpful to allow the event to raise the projected funds.

Nonprofits

Nonprofit organizations typically have staff that organize and plan events throughout the year. These events can range from "fun walks" and golf outings to black-tie dinners and annual balls. Internal staff usually juggle multiple projects at any given time under the supervision of an executive director. The planning team generally involves an honorary board and a team of volunteers. Some nonprofits recognize the value of a professional planner and will hire one to oversee the project. Another approach is to offer your services in return for visibility to the community, the executive team, and the guests at the event. These sponsorship opportunities, then, while not direct moneymakers, can provide great advertising and marketing mileage.

Another way to benefit from involvement with nonprofit organizations is to use them as training grounds. If you're in the start-up stage and feel you could use some hands-on experience, volunteering at a fund-raising run or working on planning a benefit could offer some great learning opportunities. It can be especially meaningful if you're passionate about the cause!

The Pitfalls of Event Planning

Starting a home-based event planning business is certainly not for the weakhearted. Here are some of the field's top pitfalls. Have a good look; how will you avoid these?

Not Enough Time

Owning your own business means you need time to continue your education and build your skills; time to organize your office and work environment; time to focus on sales and marketing, proposal building, and vendor networking; not to mention time spent planning events! And all of this is time away from what you were doing before this fabulous idea struck you—perhaps a full-time job or parenting. Whether you're switching careers or starting back into a career, it will take time and energy to give birth to your dream. The amount you put into your business will directly affect what you get out of it.

Incomplete Skill Set

Before you decide to start your business, you must make sure you have the necessary skills to be an effective planner. There are many seasoned professionals already in the marketplace; devel-

War Stories: Faux Pas

It's a good idea to review all the pertinent information with your staff and vendors prior to each event—right down to the names. Make sure you have people's and company's names written down, as well as their pronunciations. I've heard of event planners who posted a WELCOME sign at an event with the planner's name instead of the host company's; who announced the wrong company's name over the microphone; and who even announced the father of the bride when he'd passed away earlier that year. In some cases it's hard to be as invisible as you'd like!

Don't Be Afraid to Toot Your Own Horn!

I was nominated for Boston's Best Wedding Planner in a contest run by a local TV station. I sent an e-mail to my e-mail contact list sharing the good news and encouraged everyone to vote online. This included clients, friends, and family. As a result, a friend in my book group shared the good news with her sister, who was just starting to plan her wedding. She was beginning to feel overwhelmed by the details, was delighted to find someone familiar to help, and hired me as her planner!

oping a foothold yourself won't be easy. Be prepared to fine-tune your skills, always striving to be the best you can be. You can accomplish this by using skills gained in past jobs, through education and training, and via ongoing involvement in the industry. Be critical enough of yourself and your skills to create a business you're proud of.

Lack of Commitment

To grow a business takes commitment to your clients and the event industry. You must be prepared to take each project from start to finish; there's no room for halfhearted attempts once you've made a presentation or signed a contract. Prioritize your "to-do" list and eliminate activities that may prevent you from reaching your goals.

Lack of Knowledge

If you're not completely confident in your skills as a planner, take a step back and prepare. Volunteer, become an apprentice, take a class. Confidence can be a great asset, but evaluating your abilities honestly is even more important.

Lack of Contacts and Connections

Tell everyone you know about your exciting new plans to start your business. Scour your e-mail contact list or Palm Pilot for any people who might be able to refer business to you. The more you publicize your plans, the more real they become. And in reaching out with your ideas, your business will begin to take shape.

Trying to Do Too Much

If you've decided to start your own home-based business, now might not be the time to become a room parent, chair the PTA, or volunteer to run the school fair. Divide your day into the tasks that are necessary to grow your business, and give yourself the time to complete these tasks. I try to do the things I least enjoy first. Or the items that come due first. A friend also shared her own secret: When folks call soliciting her volunteer help, she now tells them she'll get back to them. Then she waits a day and thinks about whether the activity truly fits into her schedule.

Overpromising

Be willing to say no or refer business to a more experienced colleague if need be. Don't agree to a deadline if you aren't sure you can meet it. It's always more impressive to come in a day early than a day late when providing pricing estimates or event strategies.

Not Charging Enough for Your Services

There is no crystal ball to tell you what a customer will pay, or what you're worth. Setting your price is based on what the market will bear, your experience, and your complete understanding of the scope of the project. I will be honest and say there are times I have undercharged for my services and times I have underestimated the time needed to plan an event. In doing so, I have undercut the client's understanding of the event process and the value of a professional planner. It's true that the bidding process can sometimes leave you without options; it's all too easy to negotiate beyond a reasonable limit just to get the job. Your own experience and the state of the economy have a huge influences on pricing as well—it's a very dynamic aspect of owning a business.

Remember that you're starting a business, not a hobby. Once you know you have a service that you're proud of and are ready to go, set a price that's in line with what you're offering. Don't be afraid to charge for your time. Whether you're consulting on theme and decor, creating invitations, or running an event from start to finish, time is money. And you should be compensated for it.

Falling Behind on Business Responsibilities

Staying afloat requires ongoing attention to the financial and logistical details of each event. My suggestion is not to let things slip. Address difficult issues, contracts, or financial situations immediately and on a regular basis. This will keep you emotionally and fiscally sound.

Top Ten Mistakes in Starting Your Home-Based Event Planning Business

10. Not separating your work and home environments.

9. Not having a plan.

8. Not charging enough for your services.

7. Not being prepared to deliver what you promise.

6. Not giving clients what they ask for.

5. Not listening to what clients want.

4. Not taking all the necessary planning steps—risk assessment, contract planning, sound budget management, and so on.

3. Not saying no to a project you can't handle. (Know your limits.)

2. Not saying yes to a project you can handle. (Ask for help when needed.)

1. Not setting your professional standards high enough and reaching for them!

Not Finding the Balance between Your Business and Your Life

Your business becomes your life when you're an entrepreneur and business owner. It's hard to avoid! Still, balancing your passion for event planning with other interests will keep you refreshed and renewed. I belong to a monthly book club, for instance. I'm not always able to finish the assigned book, but I try my hardest to attend the meetings to catch up with my neighbors and friends. My husband and I share a love of music as

Ten Suggestions for Success

10. Be committed for the long haul.

9. Ask for help.

8. Learn to say no to too many responsibilities, commitments, and projects.

7. Learn to say yes to something that's challenging but that you can accomplish with success.

6. Look for opportunity—for new areas to address.

5. Don't be afraid to look at yourself critically so you can . . .

4. . . . plan the next event better than the last.

3. Say thank you.

2. Try to stay on top of your game.

1. Have fun! Enjoy what you do.

The Challenges of Event Planning

Based on what you've read so far, you can probably begin imagining the challenges of starting your own business—time, energy, knowledge, skills, marketing, growing the business, day-to-day management. . . . Take a moment now and look at some of the specifics listed below. Are you ready to do what it takes to start your own home-based business?

Dividing Your Time and Your Space

This topic is so important, I've devoted all of chapter 12 to it. It's simply vital to set guidelines for family and friends—and stick to them. Write them down, deliver them in a firm and loving voice, and make sure your loved ones know how important it is for you to follow your dream of owning your own business. Set limits on yourself, too. Go to your office when you want to work, and leave it when you're ready to stop. Be fair when determining your time commitments. If you can afford to take extra time for friends and family, do it guilt-free and love it! Remember, you'll inevitably need to ask for forgiveness and flexibility soon, when you're racing to meet a work deadline.

well and are active together in the music program at our church. No matter how difficult juggling our work and family schedules becomes in a given week, we always know we'll have this to share!

Failing to Hire Help When You Need It

Running an event from start to finish is no easy task. The fun part is developing the theme and creating the mood for the event. The hard part is hiring the right people to make it happen. You can't do it all yourself, so be ready to bring in help when you need it—even for small events. It's never too soon to start building a quality vendor directory.

Saying Yes and Saying No

If you aren't sure you should take on one more commitment, don't say yes. Think about it, consult a friend or colleague, and follow your instincts. Most people who own their own companies are doers. They're the ones who want to make things better, so they instinctively say

"Sure," "Absolutely," "I would *love* to!" But remember the other priorities in your life and face the fact that there are only twenty-four sweet hours in every day. And you do need to sleep! When you say yes, know that doing so will allow you to maintain or improve the standard of your life or the quality of the events you produce.

Pacing Yourself

Don't feel you have to do it all *now*. You don't have to buy the best equipment, go to all the networking meetings, get every degree or certification, attend every conference or training program, or handle every project that comes through your door. You also don't have to be the same event planner, friend, or volunteer that you see someone else being. We all have our own mix of priorities, capabilities, commitments, and stress-tolerance levels. Listen to yourself and your loved ones. Build your company in the way and at the pace *you* are comfortable with.

Building Your Toolbox

Your toolbox is the "guts" of your business. Work on it from the moment you head out on your own, and add to it as you gather new ideas and resources. Visit trade shows and conferences. Talk to your vendors about new products and services. Get your theme ideas from magazines and books. Stay on top of current trends to deliver new, fresh, successful events each and every time.

Should I Take the Leap?

Do I have what it takes?
- Skills
- Basic planning foundation
- Drive
- Business savvy and sense

Can I make the commitment?
- Passion
- Interest
- Independence
- Self-motivation

Can I afford to start my own business?
- Time
- Money
- Energy
- Capital investments
- Space

Am I willing to get what I need to make it work?
- Professional assistance
- Ongoing education
- Industry know-how
- Refinement of skills
- Support where it counts

Marketing

Marketing your business is an ongoing prospect. To keep your business dynamic, marketing has to be on your "to-do" list every day: One phone call. One contact. One follow-up on a lead. Just one a day will help keep the cycle going for your business. For more tips check out chapter 5, which is devoted to marketing.

Remember . . . Rome wasn't built in a day! And you don't have to build Rome. A home-based business can be as simple or as complex as you make it. It can provide you with a part-time work experience or a full-time career. And the good news is, you are in the driver's seat. You can say yes or no to business, and stop the world and get off if you so desire!

When I came into the industry in 1990, I never dreamed I would eventually plan international events or events covered by TV networks—but I have. Yet at the same time, I still find myself climbing ladders to hang swags of cloth on ceilings or tearing down the final pieces of buffet stations. It's not all glory in the end . . . but it sure is fun!

Frequently Asked Questions

Should I quit my job to start my own business?

Depending on the financial support or savings you currently have, it may make sense to begin your event business on a part-time basis. Many events can be done in the evenings or on weekends. You may be able to begin working with other seasoned planners to get your experience and once you have a solid working knowledge of the process, go out on your own. To move from a part-time to full-time commitment will take a solid client base that will guarantee repeat business and repeat income. You also need to consider the cost of health care and your fixed living expenses. Make sure your event business can offset these costs and put you in a positive cash-flow position.

I am not very organized and hate the minute details of things, but I love parties . . . can I be an event planner?

There are some basic skills that will be necessary to build a successful event planning business. Creativity is one of them, but organization and attention to detail come right behind. Building a successful business will require a good reputation and delivering excellent service. If the little details drive you crazy and you can't be bothered to figure out how to "right" the "wrongs," you may be better off filling your schedule with parties to attend, not plan. If you think you have what it takes but need some honing of skills or support in a few areas of business know-how, consider teaming up with someone who complements the skills you have.

How do I take my background in catering and launch my own event business?

It is helpful to have a background in hospitality or business if you want to focus on special events. You can take the training and experience you have and round it out with specific training in events or management from local colleges, universities, or at industry conferences.

I love all kinds of celebrations . . . what type of events should I focus on doing?

Plan to focus on the type of events that you are most comfortable with or have the most experience in. If you come from a corporate background, it may be easier for you to relate to the corporate market—and vice versa with a bride or groom if you have experience in social events. You already may know the lingo and the culture. Start with something you are familiar with and see where your successes take you. If you are chomping at the bit to make a big change, just get the training you need before taking the leap!

02

The Home Office

A Space of Your Own

The first step to starting a home-based business is having an area to work from. Start with an office setup. Perhaps you have an unfinished basement, spare room, or library that you can take over for your home office. You won't need to worry about decor or fancy furniture, but you should have a minimum of equipment and supplies to carry out the support tasks involved with creating an event.

Your office space should allow you to make phone calls uninterrupted, have enough room for you to compile proposals or file resource materials, and even allow you to store miscellaneous event supplies. If you start with a corner of your bedroom, have plans in the works to eventually move to a separate room, where you can work behind closed doors.

My first home office was set up in the basement of our first home, in a neat and tidy corner blocked in by plywood and featuring a small window to let a peek of the outside in. I went into labor with my first child while working in that office. As we changed homes, my office conditions changed, too. In one home I had the whole family room as my workspace. My family consisted of only three of us, so it was a simple feat to take over the space in its entirety.

Only once did I have less than a room. For a short period of time, a part of my bedroom housed my desk, fax, phone, and file cabinet. I will say that faxes arriving from international clients did present a level of irritation at midnight or 4:00 A.M. . . . Still, my business did extremely well. I maintained a professional image while on the phone and while traveling and produced some wonderful events for clients worldwide.

The Three Bs

When my children were small and my business was in its infancy, my rule of thumb for family interruptions when I was working was known as the three Bs. If something was burning, or someone was bleeding or not breathing . . . then they could interrupt at will. Although I have been through the experience of a child racing in to alert me to a neighbor's burning house and have taken a child to the hospital for stitches, these emergencies have been infrequent, and the client or vendor on the phone who was rudely cut off was always very understanding.

supplies, it's time to think of renting space. Still, for the small-scale home-office planner, a space in your home, set up with the necessary office supplies and equipment, will do just fine.

Equipment and Technology

Your business "starter kit" should include a telephone; answering service or machine; cell phone; computer, preferably a laptop; and a color printer. A laptop allows you to make presentations to clients as well as handle the other administrative tasks of your business. All your business functions should be automated. Get the most up-to-date technology as possible when selecting your

This setting was by no means optimal, but it did offer me a small space to organize my client and event files.

The best-case scenario is a separate room that can be closed off by a door. This isn't always possible, but it does allow you the solitude of work without interruption (if you set the rules and limits early on), and a quiet space for professional phone conversations. It helps that event planners don't usually have to meet with clients at their place of business; holding a meeting at a client's office, at a venue, or at a restaurant for lunch is quite acceptable.

If you may someday use office assistants to help with filing, proposal preparations, or event planning, a larger office would accommodate this. A converted garage, a finished basement, or a large room in your home should suffice. When you grow to the point of having several employees or need to store a large number of props or

Software Suggestions

(see Appendix D for additional contact information)

Accounting: QuickBooks, Quicken, Microsoft Small Business Accounting, NetSuite

Event Design: Vivien (room and event layout), TimeSaver, Event 411, Visio

Event Management: EventPro, Certain Software's Event Planner Plus, Caterease, PlanSoft, WynTrac (meetings and conferences)

Marketing: Photoshop, Paintshop Pro (photo manipulation)

Office Tools: Microsoft Word (letters, proposals), Access (database management), Excel (spreadsheet design), PowerPoint (presentations), FrontPage (Web site design)

Supplies: Staples, OfficeMax, Office Depot, Comp USA, Circuit City equipment. Also consider purchasing specialized programs such as QuickBooks (Intuit) for accounting, Vivien (Cast Software) for event space design, and Photoshop (Adobe) for managing photos of your events.

Marketing materials can be created using a simple word processing program, supplemented with actual photos of your events. Accounting procedures should be handled each month, including billing and budgeting. A computer fax program will let you send and receive faxes without the cost of an additional machine. I advise keeping your start-up costs down at first by learning to do these tasks yourself, using software tools easily available at your local office or computer store.

Start off using equipment and supplies you may already have in your home. As you advance in your business and have the additional income to allow for the extras, then you can go for it, but in the beginning it's wise to keep your expenses low while purchasing only those items that will give you the professional image you're looking for. I once sadly watched a colleague lose her business and her self-confidence as she struggled to pay the rent on her office and administrative staff—without having the projects to support either. By starting slowly from an office in your home, you won't be faced with choosing between your mortgage and your business rent.

As I noted previously, most people will never see what the "behind the scenes" really looks like, so don't bother spending money on fancy office furniture. If you're dying to put your personal stamp on a new purchase, my vote would be for that classic suit or jazzy outfit that really screams, *Hire me!*

What It Costs

Software:
- Basic Microsoft Office (Word, Excel, PowerPoint, Outlook): $399
- Office Professional (additional: Access, Publisher, Outlook with Business Contact Manager): $499
- Microsoft FrontPage (Web site development): $199
- Event-specific software: $99–$2,000

Equipment:
- PDA/smart phone/media: $99–$600 and up
- Computer: Desktop (with accessories) $999 and up
- Notebook: $500–$3,000
- Digital camera: $99–$2,500
- Fax (thermal/inkjet/laser): $50–$500; internal modem fax: $8–$80

Printers:
- All-in-One: printer/scanner/copier: $80–$1,000
- Inkjet: $99–$1,000
- Photo inkjet: $89–$700
- Color laser: $140–$2,540
- Laser: $130–$1,250
- Scanner: $99–$1,500

You will need a desk or table for your computer and phone, a bookshelf for storing reference materials, and suitable file cabinets for proposals, resource literature, and supplies. An additional table or area for organizing your files and proposals, or for assembling projects, is

...ll. My dining room table is often ...entral" as I assemble a hand- ...vitation or announcement or put together "goodie bags" or client incentives.

As you progress and can afford it, consider buying a scanner for adding personal event photos to your Web site or proposals, or perhaps a digital camera to snap those great event shots. Think about the least expensive way to get your point across to clients while still performing at the highest level possible. For most situations, you can take bulk copying or printing projects to a printer or an office center and eliminate the major purchase of a copier. Remember, you're an event planner, not a printer, decorator, florist, or caterer. Purchases in all areas should be limited to a few basics that you know you'll need on an ongoing basis.

Office Supplies

Your office supplies should include the basics you need to operate in a professional way. You don't need imprinted notecards or pens unless you're planning on sending an incentive gift to potential customers to announce your business opening. Try to make do with the basics to get your feet off the ground with the least amount of stress to your bank account. Start off using equipment and supplies you may already have in your home.

Business cards, stationery, and letter-sized envelopes will allow you to follow up with prospects in a consistent and professional way. Pens, notepaper, and pencils let you function in your office, draft proposals, take notes, and keep track of phone messages. Basic supplies—things like tape, glue, a stapler, and paper clips, which

Office Needs Checklist

Must have:

- Basic supplies. Pens, pencils, tape, file folders, steno books, white lined paper, ruler, stapler, self-stick notes, pencil sharpener, paper clips, business cards, letterhead, large envelopes, stickers for CD labels, envelopes
- Basic equipment. Telephone, computer, printer, fax (or fax program), cell phone

Need:

- Supplies. Paper cutter, hole punch, binders, labels, binding machine for quick professional proposals
- Services. Additional phone line, laptop computer, scanner, digital camera, DVD and CD burner, answering machine, cable or DSL Internet connection

Want:

- Copy machine
- Color laser printer
- Walkie-talkies

you may already have in your home—will need to be replaced as you use them for prospecting and projects. You'll likely need to purchase supplemental items such as file folders, labels, and large envelopes to support the organization of your office and your business. Once again, purchase and store only those items you need on a regular basis to create a professional image. Rely on a printing or office supply center for specialty items such as binding proposals or preparing large-quantity printing projects.

Event Supplies

While you don't necessarily need large quantities of props or decorations to get your business off the ground, some basic supplies and equipment will allow you to start up in a professional way. I like to have an "event toolbox" to take on every job.

This box contains items that I may need for last-minute repairs on site at an event. I also like to have a first-aid kit with me, especially for summer and outdoor outings. While you should exercise caution when administering any first aid, these miscellaneous items will often come in handy.

It's probably wise not to purchase any event equipment or decor until the first project that includes a budget for it. If you're doing a wedding and need votives, for example, it may make sense to purchase a suitable quantity and charge the client a rental fee to help offset the cost. If you foresee using these for future events as well, they will quickly pay for themselves. They are small and won't pose a huge storage problem.

Be cautious when it comes to other, larger props; it may make more sense to rent these from a decor company and purchase only the items you'll definitely reuse or can store easily. Items in my storage area include multicolored fabric for draping, miscellaneous theme tabletop decor that was unusual or unique, vases, bamboo poles, and some basic black sheer table toppers, which I now have used and reused on numerous occasions.

You must determine if you can properly store and preserve any items you decide to purchase

The Event Tool Kit

- Tape—single-sided and double-sided
- Twist-ties
- Glue gun
- Rope
- Ribbon
- Nails, screws, and tacks
- Hammer and screwdriver
- Assorted adhesives
- String
- Scissors
- Grommet maker
- Extension cords
- Camera with extra film
- Batteries
- Assorted pins (pearl-topped, T-topped, straight)
- Needle and assorted thread
- First-aid kit with Band-Aids and medical supplies
- Handi Wipes
- Sunscreen and bug spray
- Aspirin or ibuprofen

for your events. Some will go out of style, grow worn, or be damaged over time. Instead, consider this an opportunity to build up your vendor relationships; add a decor company to your team, and let them worry about the transportation, setup, and storage of themed props.

Your capital equipment checklist may also include a vehicle. Obviously, transportation to and

Software Suggestions

Caterease/Horizon Business Services
(800) 863–1616
www.caterease.com

CaterMate
(800) 486–2283
www.catermate.com

CaterPro
(916) 645–8484
www.caterprosoftware.com

Caterware
(800) 853–1017
www.caterware.com

Certain Software
(415) 353–5330
www.certain.com

Culinary Software Services
(303) 447–3334
www.culinarysoftware.com

Intuit (makers of QuickBooks, Quicken)
(800) 811–8766
www.quicken.com

NetSuite
www.netsuite.com

Party Track/Event Rental Systems
(877) 967–3984
www.partytrack.com

PlanSoft
(330) 405–5555
www.plansoft.com

ReNTiT
(800) 621–2495

ReServe Interactive/Efficient Frontiers
(888) 4–EFI–SALES
www.efficient-frontiers.com

Ruth Meric's Party Perfect Catering
& Event Software
(800) 522–5440
www.partyperfect.net

Synergy International
(800) 522–6210
www.synergy-intl.com

TimeSaver Software
(888) 877–1100
www.timesaversoftware.com

Vivien
www.viviendesign.com

WynTrac
(877) WYNTRAC
www.wyntrac.com

from your events is essential, but a new cargo van isn't. I occasionally rent a van when I have a lot of supplies to transport. For most events and sales calls, though, my Grand Cherokee, fresh from the car wash, is just fine. If you live in the city, public transportation might provide you with all you need to get yourself going in business.

The important thing, as always, is to present yourself in a professional way; this is a point worth repeating! If you can do this with supplies you already have, rather than making a large investment in these early days, you'll be much better off financially.

Frequently Asked Questions

I am ready to launch my business! Why shouldn't I take a five-year lease out at the most prestigious office park to really get attention for my business and start out on the right foot?

Unless you have had a recent inheritance or have large sums of money buried in your backyard, it is wise to start slowly. Most clients will not need to have meetings at your office, so in the beginning it is wise to spend your start-up costs on office equipment, specific event supplies, or education to get you up and running.

What software will I need to get started?

Check out appendix D and the Software Suggestions sidebar to get a good idea of the options out there. There are many programs that will help with basic office support and, more specifically, event planning and logistics. They range in cost from nothing to thousands of dollars. My advice would be to start slow. Try to get a trial version of the software and use it to see if it suits your needs. You may find that you use it too seldom to warrant the price, or one of your vendors may have a more sophisticated version that they can support you with. If you can envision yourself using it to support your sales or planning, consider charging a small administration fee on each job to help offset the cost.

Do I need a separate phone/fax line?

Absolutely! Being able to clearly know what call is for business is essential in putting forth a professional image. If you add an additional line to your home, you will not get business support and any extras such as toll-free options, but it will be less expensive. Taking out a full business line may give you some Internet or additional features that will help your marketing efforts as well. Some fax services offer online products, eliminating an additional phone line for faxes. Check with your local phone service provider for benefits and features that best suit your needs.

Where could I have an alternate meeting site for client appointments? My home office just doesn't seem professional enough!

It's a good idea to have a couple of places that are professional and accessible for client meetings. I often meet at a hotel that I do work with, and they are happy to give me a room to set up any centerpieces, show my portfolio, or have a light lunch or coffee with a client. Sometimes even a coffee shop that is comfortable and trendy can set the atmosphere you want to create for your new business. Some areas have community offices where, for a small monthly fee, you can utilize a central conference area and even have a company name listed on an entrance directory. In any case, opt for a professional location that allows you to put your best foot forward.

03

Developing Your Business

Your Business Structure

The next step to bringing your business to life is to formalize it. What kind of business will it be? What will you call it? Are you going it alone or joining forces with a colleague and forming a partnership? Where do you start?

First, do some research. Scour your local library for information on starting a business. Government agencies such as the U.S. Small Business Administration are also great resources. Most cities have a local SBA office; or you can visit them online at www.sba.gov. Local business groups or your chamber of commerce can provide helpful tips, too.

Take a look at business plans of friends or of other small businesses. Don't be afraid to ask advice from retired business owners. Contact your local office of SCORE, "Counselors to America's Small Business," for more information or the names of members who can offer guidance. You may find a mentor who can walk you through all the details of small-business setup and management.

The type of business structure you choose will affect how you are taxed and the type of record keeping you must do. Running the business as a sole proprietor is the simplest, most informal arrangement; incorporating, on the other hand, poses more financial record keeping but also greater asset protection. If you have a colleague who shares your dream and enthusiasm for starting a home-based business, then a formal partnership might be your best business structure option. There are pros and cons to each structure, so think it over carefully. In any case, I recommend consulting with an attorney who can help answer questions and guide you through the process.

Let's take a look at the options.

Sole Proprietorship

This is the most common form of business ownership. One person owns all of the assets and liabilities. The owner has exclusive control of the business but also total financial responsibility to the full extent of the assets of the business as well as the owner's personal assets. It's relatively simple to complete the documents necessary to set up a sole proprietorship, once a name search is done. If the name of the business is not the same as the name of the owner, a "Doing Business As" (DBA) certificate must be filed in the city or town hall where the business is conducted.

Pros: You have exclusive control of your company, and the setup process is simple. You also receive all the income.

Cons: You're liable for all financial obligations to the extent of all your business *and* personal assets. You may not deduct medical benefits as a business expense.

General Partnership

Starting a partnership would mean finding a kindred spirit who shares your drive and passion for the business. It also should be someone whom you work well with, who balances your business style, and who is willing to approach the business in a serious manner. You and your partner (or partners) will be sharing in the profits as well as the losses of the business, according to your respective ownership interests. Partners owe each other the duty of utmost good faith and loyalty.

The relationship is governed by a written agreement if you and your partner have one, and if not, it's governed by statutory provisions. DBA certificates must also be filed, and a separate tax identification number obtained from the IRS.

A limited liability partnership is the same as a general partnership, except some states permit one partner to limit liability caused by another's negligence or breach of contract toward the investment in the partnership. Each partner is still liable to the full extent of his or her personal assets for liabilities incurred.

In a limited partnership, the general partner has full liability and management of the business; limited partners have limited management. Their liability is limited to their investment in the business. A joint venture is organized for a brief time and a specific event. If the relationship or activities continue after the initial engagement, a general partnership should be formed.

Pros: Partners can divide up the work, including sales, administration, and site visits. They can cover each other during vacations and illness. They can work together to take on larger, more complicated projects. While the partnership must file a tax return, it pays no income taxes—the profits and losses flow from the partnership return to each partner's individual tax return.

Cons: Liability is still an issue. Each partner is personally liable for any obligation incurred by another partner. Thus, you are responsible to the full extent of your personal assets for any liability incurred by another partner, through contract or negligently causing someone injury, whether or not you had anything to do with it or even knowledge of it. Partners may find that they don't get along, making it difficult to carry on the business. You also need to clearly define everyone's roles and anticipate what will happen to the business in the event that any partner ceases to work due to disability, death, or otherwise.

Incorporation

By incorporating your business, you form a legal entity solely for the purpose of conducting business. A person or group of people forms the business entity and elects a board of directors to control the company. This board in turn can elect officers to run the business on a daily basis. Many corporations are closely held, meaning that the shareholders also serve as the board of directors and officers. The corporate entity itself becomes the business, not the individuals who run it. Ordinarily, a corporation bears a separate burden for taxes and liabilities.

Pros: The main benefit of incorporating is the avoidance of personal liability. If a lawsuit should be filed against you, the corporation would be held responsible, not you individually.

Medical benefits may be deducted. A subchapter S election can be taken, allowing earnings to be taken as distributions and passed through your personal tax return.

Cons: Record keeping becomes more detailed, and the fees for running a corporation are higher. Articles of Organization must be filed with and approved by a state government, as must annual reports with attendant filing fees. Bylaws must be adopted and followed, along with minutes of meetings.

Limited Liability Company (LLC)

This is also a separate business entity created by the provisions of special state laws. It's similar to a corporation but without some of the limitations; your attorney should be able to spell out this structure thoroughly if you feel you would benefit from it.

Pros: Profits and losses are noted on individual tax returns, but the LLC is held responsible for any liability issues.

Cons: Much as with a corporation, an LLC requires more record keeping than a sole proprietor or partnership.

Once you've laid the foundation, take a look at what you'll construct on it. Put it in writing. As an event planner, you know the importance of planning, so start the planning process with your own business. What kind of event planning services will you provide? Only if you identify your goals clearly from the start will you be able to chart your successes and make the necessary changes along the way to ensure you reach your goals.

Business Planning 101: Market Research

Getting a sense for your business potential is essential. Before you take the plunge, test the water. A thorough and honest investigation of the viability of an event planning business in your geographic area or in your select specialty area will help you start off on the right foot. Your research may even uncover information that will help you focus your business strategies and save you from costly and time-consuming mistakes.

Identify the Competition

Check your yellow pages for event planners in your area. Read business journals, specialty magazines, and newsletters looking for event advertisers in your area. Research online for providers and their marketing techniques. What can you offer that is different? How can you put a spin on your company to create more interest or create a niche market? Identify whom you are up against and prepare yourself to go into battle well informed.

Identify Industry Growth Potential

Read up on how events are treated in today's economy. When you present your services, you must make sure you do so in an appropriate way. In the 1990s events were lavish and over the top. We saw Web site premieres, launch parties, and client events that kept getting bigger and better. Budgets were created to support events that represented how much people cared about the way they entertained their guests.

In the early twenty-first century, the focus changed as wallets tightened. Likewise, the events that were created had to reflect the prudence people were showing in their daily lives. Still fun events, but scaled back. Being tuned in to the whys of an event will allow you do the hows in an appropriate way. This will get you business and keep it coming back.

Identify Potential Markets

As you scan the Web or read up on business opportunities, look for areas that are ripe for event services. Match this with your interests and skills. If your local business pages or event directories show a slew of wedding planners but no planners for children's events, take note. If a nearby community seems ripe to hire event planners given its changing demographics, take a closer look at focusing here. Markets could be based on geographic territories, types of services, types of customers, or even budget levels. Planning fifteen smaller events might bring as much income and satisfaction as two large events.

Identify and Quantify Market Share

You have decided you must stay in your 50-mile radius and limit yourself to social events. You know who your competitors are. Now take an honest look at what business they are getting and what would be left for you. Is there something they're missing that you could provide? Are they handling all the country club events, for instance, but none of the hotel events? Develop your checklist of potential clients and event locations, and start doing your homework. This will give you a sense for your opportunities. Remember, it takes time to develop business; be consistent and persistent with your efforts.

Identify Your Strengths and Opportunities for Success

As you begin your research, you'll see where your forte may lie. If you're coming from a corporate background, you may be comfortable dealing with professional clients. Or perhaps your background is more on the social end, and planning celebratory events would suit you better. Do you enjoy the excitement of children's or community events? If you can find an area you love and are good at, this would be the place to start.

Consider Your Marketing Plan

How will you get your business off the ground and running? Chapter 5 will walk you through the creation of your marketing plan in depth, but it's wise to start thinking about it now. Start a database of contacts, and keep track of your initial calls and plans for follow-up. It takes effort to develop a relationship with a client, so be prepared to pay your dues. Drop potential clients a note in the mail periodically. Develop a personalized incentive item with your company name on it to remind folks of what you do. Tie it in with the type of event service you'll be offering.

Business Planning 102: Selecting a Business Identity

Now that you've done your research and thought about your plan of attack, it's time to put it in writing.

The Business Name

In selecting your business name, be sure to do your research and settle on something unique. Your attorney can run a check locally and nationally to make sure any name you're considering isn't already taken. Also check out existing Web addresses: You'll want to use your company name

Sample Business Names—Pros and Cons

Events by Ellen	This shows that you do events but not specifically what kind.
Parties to Go	This lets people know you provide party services with some sort of portability option.
Corporate Events, Inc.	No mistaking what this company does!
Designing Divas	A partnership of creative designers—but what kind?
John Smith Events	Seems reasonable, but make sure there are no other John Smith event planners out there!
Fabulous Events, Inc.	Clearly an event company— catchy but not too trendy.

as your Web site for optimal exposure and to help new clients locate you easily.

When I selected my company name—*J. S. Moran & Associates, event planning & management*—I wanted my identity to be tied into my company name and added the descriptor words to identify what type of business I was. I later updated my company name to *jsmoran, special event planning & management*. My Web site address is www.jsmoran.com, and the subtitle allowed me to reach out to a social client looking for a celebration or a corporate client wanting planning support. This covers the need to clearly identify who I am and what I do.

There are many options for great names. The important thing is to select something you can live with for the long run and that isn't already being used by someone else. Once your attorney has done the research, you can file the appropriate papers both locally and nationally to protect your investment. You will be spending time, energy, and money to publicize your company; you don't want to find out you're being sued by someone who already registered your name!

The Business Logo

A logo can be a great way to market your identity visually. It can be created from a combination of letters in your name or be a symbol that represents the style or type of events you specialize in. When creating a logo, you will need to work with a professional graphic designer who will create what you are looking for and work with you to complement your business cards, letterhead, or brochure material. You will incur some up-front

costs for this, but once you have your logo finalized, you'll have it on disc to reproduce in the future on marketing materials such as proposals, incentive items, or wearables for your planning team.

If you think about the many products and services you use and the logos associated with them, you'll understand the impact a logo can have. When you see a logo, a company immediately comes to mind. Consider the long-term viability of your selection and ask for the advice of your graphic designer. You will want to select something that speaks of the flavor of your business. Whether it be classic, whimsical, fun, or modern . . . select an image that you feel will withstand the test of time and reflects the heart of your business.

The Business Plan

Now you're ready for the key element: Your business plan. This is a document that formalizes your dream of owning your own business. It'll

Business Plan Basics

Mission statement

Objectives

Credentials (your résumé)

Organizational chart

Marketing plan

Operations plan

Financial plan

also be the measurement tool by which you can evaluate your success. Although you probably won't be presenting this plan to potential investors, or even showing it to clients or colleagues, nevertheless having it will give you direction and confidence: You have both goals and a way to reach them. As you move through the inevitable changes in your business, look at your business plan from time to time to see if you're still aiming in the right direction.

What goes into a business plan? What follows is a rundown of a good plan's most important elements, along with some samples to help you get started.

Mission Statement

What is the purpose of your business? Create a short, concise statement that you can deliver and build your business on. This might include your values and offer keys to success. It will also allow you to stand out from the crowd and reveal how your services differ from the competition.

Sample mission statement:

jsmoran, special event planning & management, is a full-service special event company focusing on corporate and celebratory events worldwide. We position ourselves as a resource to nonprofit and corporate management teams to support growth through the flawless execution of special events and meetings. We help groups and individuals create unique and memorable events through creative planning and professional execution.

Objectives

What are the objectives of your business? Why are you offering your services? What will you provide to your clients to improve the quality of their lives? This information can be added to your Web site and your marketing materials; it can also be used to measure how well you've satisfied your clients' needs.

Sample objectives:

The objectives of my business are:

To design, execute, and evaluate events or meetings that support and promote social celebrations, marketing efforts, or internal or educational programs.

To offer a worldwide presence with events/meetings presented at major trade show cities or international venues, at company locations, or at specialized venues.

To offer a valuable service to company planning teams, directors, and those responsible for creating events with professional advice and experience that will help streamline the process, save money, and create dynamic experiences.

Types of events include:

Trade-show-related events	Grand openings
Product launches	Company outings
Client incentive events	Award dinners
	Web site premiere events
Educational and user meetings	Commemorative events
Golf outings	Social celebrations
	Recruitment events

Credentials

What qualifies you to start an event planning business? The "Credentials" section of your business plan is where you must take an honest look at what you bring to your work. Just enjoying parties won't cut it. You should have a track record of event planning, have experience within the hospitality industry, or have worked in an event-related industry dealing with the planning process. You may need to build on what you have in order to sell yourself as a full-service planner. Decide where the gaps in your training are, and set out to fill them.

Your "Credentials" section should list all the jobs or activities that have led you to your decision to start your own business. Also describe your plans to build on and enhance the experience you already have: the courses or programs you'll enroll in, any certifications you plan to get, and the educational conferences you can commit to attending. This will show that you're motivated to be the best and will be savvy to the most current trends and event services. As an active member of the industry, you will ensure that your customers receive state-of-the-art advice by using the most up-to-date products and themes.

The biography below shows a solid balance of basic knowledge backed by an understanding of what is necessary to complete training as a self-employed event professional. This self-examination, coupled with a team of solid business professionals, could start you on your way.

Sample credentials:

Having been the event coordinator for a top five-star resort, I have covered all aspects of coordinating special events within a specific venue. I have worked with existing clients who are holding meetings within the facility and have produced special events representing a variety of creative themes.

I have interfaced with food service managers to create menus, worked with in-house audiovisual services to provide sound, and hired outside production and prop companies to carry out my theme ideas. I have built a file of contacts for many event support services, including graphic designers, florists, balloon artists, and entertainment providers.

While I have been responsible for many of the planning procedures, I have not had direct selling responsibility or the opportunity to work in a variety of venues or with a variety of caterers. There are some services I am unfamiliar with, such as transportation companies and tent companies.

I plan to enhance my expertise by attending an upcoming conference and specifically selecting courses that will round out my knowledge. As a member of my local ISES chapter, I will seek out additional vendor support and get referrals on reliable services from my colleagues. I will also enroll in the study course to become a Certified Special Events Professional and aim for certification within two years.

Organizational Chart

How will your business be managed? This will be based on its formal structure. If you are the sole proprietor, you will be the CEO or president. You can identify your support team as the group of professionals who help you reach your business goals—whether or not they're employees of your company.

In chapter 6, I'll offer suggestions on developing your team, including vendors and support staff. For most home-based event planning businesses, the organizational chart is fairly simple: It shows the owner and professional staff, with most services provided by trusted vendors.

Sample organizational chart:

CEO and president: Patty Planner, PBC
Duties: Business management, sales, marketing

Accounting: Doug Detail, CPA
Duties: Financial management including tax planning

Legal: Larry Lawyer, Esquire
Duties: Legal issues including contracts

Marketing Plan

Here you state how you'll launch your business. This is the path from your heart to your customer. Nothing happens without a sale, so this is a crucial stepping-stone to getting your business off and running. After doing your research, decide on your focus market and go for it. You may include an array of strategies including direct mailings, advertising, and cold calling. Remember that this may change as economic or local business conditions evolve. Be prepared to review and update as necessary.

Sample marketing plan:

To reach out to customers, I will become an active member of the Greater Boston Convention and Visitors Bureau and become a useful resource for the business community. I will achieve prominence and recognition by attending monthly meetings and by following up on business contacts and leads promptly.

I will also join at least two professional organizations and offer to serve on a committee. This will give me recognition in the community and afford me lead opportunities as well as professional growth.

I will direct my sales efforts to specific markets and create a strong campaign that clearly defines my skills and the benefits of using my services. This marketing campaign will include developing a Web site, a brochure that will be sent to my target market, and a quarterly postcard with seasonal information. All direct-mail pieces will be followed up with a personal telephone contact and periodic checks to pursue opportunities.

Operations Plan

Broadly identify the many ways in which you'll facilitate an event. Begin building a directory of vendors who will support your events. This will also show your understanding of what's involved with the event process and serve to broaden your support base.

Your support team can include invitation designers, caterers, florists, rental companies, production and lighting companies, decor and prop houses, and general staffing support. By incorporating these vendors into your plan, you lay the foundation to carry out your creative ideas.

Sample operations plan:

As a full-service event planning company, I will offer strategic planning, design and execution, vendor management, and evaluation. The daily operations team will consist of a project manager who will interact directly with clients and oversee all aspects of the planning. Appropriate and unique vendors will be secured to supply all necessary components of the event; professional staff will support all levels of planning, including administrative, staffing, and professional services.

The team will be prepared to offer twenty-four-hour service when needed for weekend and evening events; members will be available via cell phone and pager to address all client and vendor needs. The day-to-day operations will be driven from office headquarters with a master resource file listing pertinent vendor contact information. Timelines and production schedules will drive the execution of events and provide valuable benchmarks for monitoring success.

Financial Plan

Before you start daydreaming about cashing the first big check from your first big client, consider what you need to do to get to this point. What funds will you need to start your company? How will you pay for your office supplies and marketing materials? How will you cover your operational costs? Most service-based businesses do not require a great deal of start-up funding. The items you need can usually be purchased with savings, bought on credit, or postponed until your sales allow for such expenses. Be careful not to overspend in the early start-up stages—wait until your cash flow allows for additional purchases for your business.

Sample financial plan:

In the initial start-up phase of my planning business, I will utilize existing space in my home for office and administrative duties and will invest in a new computer and printer, paid

---

What It Costs

Professional Fees

Attorney: $150–$350 per hour

Accountant: $500–$2,000 consulting/tax returns

Bookkeeper: $25–$50 per hour

Graphic designer: $25–$125 per hour, $500–$1,500 per project

Web designer: $25–$150 per hour, $200–$2,500 per site

---

for on credit. Additional expenses in the start-up phase will include the services of a graphic artist to assist with marketing materials, including Web site, stationery, and logo development. These will be financed through savings, with ongoing funding of additional services paid for by event income when and if funds are available.

Setting Goals

The final segment of your business planning involves setting business goals, both short term and long term. What are you setting your sights on for this month, this year? Once you've mapped out your long-term goals, then you can break them down into the weekly tasks that will allow you to achieve them.

Short-Term Goals

Getting new business might be one short-term goal. Setting up your office might be another. Keeping your vendor list fresh, gathering new

Short-Term Goal: Secure a Wedding Client in Three Months

Week 1:

- Contact ten associates and ask for a referral.
- Drop a note to friends and family saying hello and sharing your dream.
- Make appointments with five wedding facilities to tour the property in exchange for sharing your service presentation.
- Take out an ad in a wedding guide.
- Write an article on "Ten Steps to a Stress-Free Wedding Day."
- Drop off business cards at bridal shops, caterers' offices, and florists.

Week 2:

- Follow up with sales efforts.
- Create new contact lists if no positive responses are received.
- Make appointments with brides.
- Attend bridal fairs for ideas and leads.
- Exhibit at local bridal fairs.
- Contact wedding venues to showcase at any open houses.

Week 3:

- Follow up with sales efforts.
- Make appointments with brides.
- Send and sign contracts.
- Start planning.

Week 4:

- Continue responding to inquiries from ads.
- Follow up with venues and vendors.
- Follow up with potential brides.
- Continue planning events under contract.

Weeks 5–8:

- Same as above: Call, contact, and follow up.
- Respond to all inquiries.
- Make appointments with potential clients.
- Keep the planning process going.
- Hire help as your wedding business begins to boom!

Weeks 9–12:

- Continue to incorporate prospecting for business into weekly goals.
- Continue to manage new appointments.
- Continue the planning process with booked business.

event ideas, or preparing an article for a newspaper could be added to the list. Once you've determined your goals, you can work backward to create a timeline allowing you to meet them.

Long-Term Goals

Your long-term goals are an extension of your short-term goals. By achieving goals on a monthly basis, you can look at what you are accomplishing over time. Long-term goals tend to be more general and broader in scope. They are less specific and task oriented and more results oriented. As I noted above, breaking down the long-term goals into smaller components will show you how to achieve the results you're looking for in a series of manageable steps.

Your long-term goals are the vision that keeps you going through the ups and downs of your business. As the entrepreneur, you will deliver this vision to your clients, vendors, and staff as you offer your services.

Here are some examples of long-term goals:

- To create a business that I can sell in ten years
- To plan events in ten major cities within a five-year period
- To become a leader in an international organization
- To become recognized as one of the top five planners in my city
- To develop a strong social event planning company creating two events per month
- To grow my business to five employees
- To become certified within five years

To reach these goals, you can use your short-term timeline to break each dream into weekly steps. These may include education, volunteerism, and investing time and money. They will be achieved by the work you do on a daily basis to build your business and reputation. Be prepared to change them as your situation changes. The economy, business trends, and your lifestyle may create a dynamic environment for your business. Still, if you don't set goals, you'll never reach them.

Frequently Asked Questions

Should I team up with a friend or go it alone?

It depends on how much time you have to put into your business; if you need the help, motivation, or support of a co-worker; if you can trust and depend on your partner-to-be; if you share the same work ethic, passion, and financial motivation; and if you have a good gut feeling about going into business with this friend. It takes a special relationship built on honesty, flexibility, shared vision, and commitment to make a partnership work. But for some people, the support and camaraderie of a partner can make, not break, the success of a new business. A good rule of thumb is to be careful when partnering with family or friends; it could put your relationship on shaky grounds. Go into business in a professional way with another professional. Go into it in writing, laying out all the details of your business partnership.

Is it worth it to pay for marketing lists or to enlist a company to do market research for me?

In most cases, you will learn a great deal from digging into your market and doing the research on your own. Even though it is time-consuming, you may learn more about what areas of events really interest you and will be most financially or personally rewarding, and you may actually uncover markets that you never knew existed! Resources such as business journals that generate yearly compilations of industry-specific lists with contact numbers, names, and addresses can be extremely helpful if you are planning an e-mail or a postcard blast or are doing a press release.

How do I decide on a name for my company? Do I need a logo?

Choosing a company name can be very personal. It can also be expensive if you decide to print marketing materials and then realize the look isn't working for you. Spend some time brainstorming and get input and comments from friends, family, or clients. Everyone will have their own preference on look and feel, but try to choose something that fits your style and has endurance. Try to stay away from trendy or overly specific titles that will become outdated or limit you if you decide to expand or diversify.

Do I really need to write a business plan or detail out my goals?

Absolutely. Even though it seems painful and needless to write the details down, it will help you to formalize and create a path that will lead you to success! By detailing the step-by-step plan you will make, you can begin to check off your successes and see the holes or gaps that may arise that will keep you from achieving your goals.

04

Dollars and Sense

Determine how you can grow your business and stay financially sound from the start. Will you be leaving full-time employment or fitting in events on weekends or evenings? How will you manage your income and expenses and track your projects? In any case, from your very first project you should approach the process in a professional and businesslike way. This will help you during the planning stages, at billing time, and—most importantly—as you evaluate the profitability of your business.

Tracking Your Business

There are many great general business accounting programs available now. I have used QuickBooks for many years. It's simple to use and complete enough for me to track projects. I complement the program with a separate spreadsheet on which every expense is logged. If I prepare a budget estimate, I follow up on it by tracking each subsequent purchase, creating addendums if needed. The program you select should allow you to invoice your clients, pay your bills, and track expenses and income. It should also give you a snapshot of the financial health of your company and assist you in your legal and tax responsibilities.

The Cash-Flow Statement

A cash-flow statement is a useful tool in observing how money flows in and out each month. Here's why: The event planning business can be very seasonal; you may have slow times and frantic times throughout the year. Unfortunately, expenses often occur on a routine basis—think

Cash Flow Projections

	Jan	Feb	Mar	April	May	June	July	August	Sept	Oct	Nov	Dec	Total
INCOME													
Weddings						$5,000	$5,000	$5,000	$5,000				$20,000
Holiday parties											$5,000	$5,000	$10,000
Fund-raisers		$5,000	$5,000										$10,000
Summer outings					$5,000	$5,000	$5,000						$15,000
Total Income All Projects													**$55,000**
EXPENSES													
Professional dues and publications							$800						$800
Office supplies	$50			$50			$50			$50		$50	$250
Vehicle	$600	$600	$600	$600	$600	$600	$600	$600	$600	$600	$600	$600	$7,200
Tax payments				$2,500									$2,500
Insurance	$800												$800
Telephone	$120	$120	$120	$120	$120	$120	$120	$120	$120	$120	$120	$120	$1,440
Equipment	$50	$50	$50	$50	$50	$50	$50	$50	$50	$50	$50	$50	$600
Industry conferences	$800							$800					$1,600
Travel	$1,000							$1,000					$2,000
Marketing expenses	$200												$200
Printing	$200						$200						$400
Postage		$100						$100					$200
Shipping													
Entertainment	$50	$50	$50	$50	$50	$50	$50	$50	$50	$50	$50	$50	$600
Total Expenses													**$18,590**

of your costs for your telephone, vehicle, advertising, office supplies, and so on. By being aware of the flow of cash, though, you can keep a firm grasp on your finances at all times.

The cash-flow statement also allows you to make observations on how to create a more even flow of money in and out of your business bank account. Perhaps you target holiday events to complement summer outings. If you're a wedding planner, the winter may be a slow time, but you could enhance your services to offer holiday stationery or in-home decorating or party assistance.

The cash-flow statement model on page 42 shows the finances of an event planner working on a mix of corporate and social accounts. You should be able to generate similar statements from the accounting software program you choose.

Take an honest look at what you would spend to maintain a professional business on a yearly basis and start from there. If you know that to operate your business, for example, you'll need $20,000, then plan on securing at least twice that amount of business to cover all expenses and taxes. Partner this analysis with your marketing plan to make your business work!

Bank Accounts

It's imperative that you keep all your business transactions separate from your personal accounts. It'll help you enormously at tax time and validate that you're running a home-based business, as well as keeping your image sharp and professional. You can do this by opening up a business checking account and using this for all business transactions. You should likewise have a business credit card to use for charging business-related expenses.

You may also want to open up a few store or vendor accounts to begin to build credit relationships with suppliers. Write these bills using your business checking account to keep things organized and running professionally. Even when you want to withdraw funds from your business account, write a check to yourself to help you track your personal deductions from the business.

Tax and Financial Planning

The tax responsibilities and record keeping required of a home-based business are drastically different from those for an individual. A meeting with your accountant will help you set up a system that you can stick with throughout the year and make tax preparations run that much smoother.

As a rule of thumb, consider setting aside 40 percent of all of the income from consulting fees. Keep a fund in your savings account to make quarterly tax payments that represent an appropriate tax burden, so you will not be faced with a huge bill on April 15. Your quarterly estimates will be based on the prior year's earnings, but if you're having a banner year, it will be important to prepare for a larger tax hit by tucking the money away during the year.

Business expenses will offset your tax exposure, but not all expenses will be deducted directly from your gross income. Consult your accountant if you feel your conditions are changing. He or she will best advise you on how to plan throughout the year.

Show Me the Money: Pricing Your Services
The Budget

For any given project a budget is created. This includes the client's available or allotted funds, the project's scope, the number of attendees, and the breadth of services. I will go over budget components in more detail later in this chapter, but I think it's helpful to open our discussion of pricing with a sample budget:

Birthday Party Bash

Decor	
Production services: lighting, sound, decor, draping, labor	$7,200
Rentals: high cocktail tables	$100
Table linens, decor, and centerpieces	$800
Balloons	$500
Flooring	$950
Invitations	$3,500
Photography	$1,500
Catered cuisine	$4,200
Subtotal	**$18,750**
Planning fees: concept, design, coordination, planning, setup, and on-site management (20% of project)	$3,750
Estimated Total	**$22,500**

As you can see, I feel that an allowance for planning fees is a crucial part of a budget. When you agree to perform the planning services, you must commit to carrying the project to fruition with all the components you've presented or that the client has requested. You should estimate the time it will take to manage this process from start to finish and bill accordingly.

By pricing your services properly, you will approach the project in a positive and professional manner and the client will see the value in using your services. If you underprice, you risk not giving the project your full attention, because you can't afford to. If you overprice, you risk losing customers if they realize they're being unfairly treated. In any case, careful consideration must be given to the scope of the project and the time you'll put into it. As you progress through the planning, this will also help you in constructing your timeline and project overview.

Pricing by Percentage

One way to estimate the cost of your services is to figure your cost as a percentage of the total budget. I try to use 20 to 25 percent of the total as a benchmark. This is not always how the final numbers flush out, but it is a starting point. Negotiations sometimes come into play. If you're taking on a project in part to gain exposure or contacts, you might want to make more allowances in pricing. On the other hand, if you sense that a client will be needing more than the typical amount of hand-holding, then think about fee-for-services or hourly rate pricing.

Pricing by Fee for Services

If, during the proposal stages, you get the impression that the project will require additional meetings, ongoing changes, updated progress reports, or the like, you may want to clearly define what you will do for the set fee and offer the option of additional hours at an hourly rate. This rate would be based, as in many professional industries, on experience and qualifications.

When drafting your proposal, estimate how much time it will take for basic administrative duties, event coordination, marketing and promotion, and risk assessment and management. Break down each category into the components you'll be covering and the estimated time it will take to carry out the tasks. This will give you a starting point for what you might charge for a planning fee.

Let's take a look at some examples. You are given a budget of $50,000 for a 200-guest event. If you get a sense that the event will be relatively easy to manage—say, it's held at a local country club that you work with on a regular basis; the food service will be handled internally; there will be no rentals, transportation, or outside security or lighting needed; and the only additional services will be decor—then you may be able to charge a flat fee that will cover roughly thirty hours of planning time.

On the other hand suppose the event will be held 100 miles away. It will also need tenting as well as full rentals of tables, chairs, linens, lighting, and power—and you've been asked to coordinate outside services such as entertainment, photography, video, and florals. In this case you'll want to project a much higher fee. Consider travel time, telephone and correspondence time for all vendors, and multiple updates for time-

War Stories: Don't Count Your Chickens . . .

An event colleague, eager to produce a fundraising event for a local church, agreed to hire a caterer, entertainers, and rentals for a summer fete in return for a portion of the money raised from the event. Unfortunately, the weather was bad, turnout was poor, and the caterer charged an agreed-upon minimum for food services. The planner was out $10,000 as a result of her optimism. *A word of caution:* Be realistic and fiscally responsible with your business funds!

lines and production schedules. In this instance your quote may include 130 or more hours for planning.

You may also figure in a range of planning expenses based on delegating some of the tasks for which you would pay a variety of fees. You may know you can pay an assistant at $10 per hour to handle clerical tasks, favor assembly, and on-site setup, while a higher fee would be assigned for creative design and event management. Figuring in the variety of fees, you will arrive on a final project cost to cover your time and labor.

Pricing by the Hour

Using the same projection format, you may decide to present an hourly fee structure and tie each action item into a cost line. This gives the client a clear picture of what it takes to carry an event to fruition and allows you to be compensated for your time appropriately. You may have to negotiate your time or make alterations based on budgets. It will be up to you, the professional, to educate your clients as to the value of your services. If you're pricing your services out of their budget, think about eliminating items that could be performed by the clients or their staff and focusing on the tasks that are integral to the planning process.

The range for hourly fees could be as low as $25 per hour or as high as $125, depending on the type of task and the consultative value you'll bring to the table. Remember, you'll be paying for your own benefits, Social Security, and taxes out of the hourly rate you receive, so don't underestimate your worth.

Pricing by Commissionable Rates/Add-Ons

In some instances I have seen proposals with no line item for planning fees. The planner is compensated by adding a "handling fee" or "finder's fee" to all the services that are provided at the event. If you'll be managing the rentals, florals, linens, and so forth, you may be eligible for a volume discount, which you could take as a commission. The client will not know what this amount is but should realize this is being done if there is no indication that you're being paid clearly printed on the estimate or invoice. In this case you would handle all the billing, submitting the total invoice to the client if asked to, and reducing the amount paid to the vendor by the agreed-upon percentage.

I personally try to avoid this method. I feel that it's important to show my value to clients with a line item on the invoice. I also pass discounts on to them, showing them the savings that they will realize by enlisting my services and using my power of purchase. I think this is a much stronger way to showcase the professionalism of the industry.

Negotiating with Clients

There are times when the price you think you should get just doesn't match what the market will bear. Negotiations sometimes—though not always—come into play as you move from the proposal to the contract stage. You'll want to use your professional judgment to determine whether you want to negotiate. It depends on how much you want the business, the difficulty you'll have executing the event, and what marketing value the event might bring to you. Even if you do elect to discount your price, I advise always listing the total value of the event on your contract to give clients a clear picture of a planner's worth. From that number, you may deduct a percentage or a flat amount to reach a mutually agreeable price.

Negotiating with Vendors

You can negotiate with vendors for more attractive pricing. If you can foresee using a vendor for multiple events, you might be able to set up a "quantity discount." You would pass this on to each individual client to highlight the value of using a professional planner. Try to be sensitive about the suppliers' need to cover their own costs. Fixed-cost items may be easier for a vendor to discount than disposable or high-maintenance items that require repair, cleaning, or labor. Relationships with vendors are often a delicate balancing act, and it's important to always respect

jsmoran

1 Event Way

Celebrate, ON 54321

Invoice

DATE	INVOICE #
8/2/2007	PH15

Bill To

P.O. NO.	TERMS	PROJECT

QUANTITY	DESCRIPTION	RATE	AMOUNT
		Total	$0.00

Date:			Corporate Summer Outing			Venue A		
		number of guests		pp price			total	
Adult menu		125		$ 34.45	pp		$	4,306.25
Children's menu		40		$ 12.00	pp		$	480.00
	Total						$	**4,786.25**
	20	Soft drinks		$ 1.50	each		$	30.00
	45	Water		$ 1.50	each		$	67.50
	329	Bar beverages		$ 3.50			$	1,151.50
		Bar gratuity						
							$	6,035.25
Gratuity				n/a				
							$	6,035.25
		Sales tax			5%		$	301.76
Subtotal food & beverage							$	6,337.01
Park admission fee: under 3 years old								
Electrical outlet							$	65.00
Boat rentals	5	Paddleboat rental		$ 85.00			$	425.00
Boat rentals	5	Canoe rental		$ 65.00			$	325.00
Bartenders		Beer/wine/margs					$	125.00
Waterfront							$	300.00
Facility rental							$	1,500.00
Total facility charges							$	9,077.01
Entertainment & decor items								
Disc jockey & game show							$	2,700.00
Decor: balloons, tabletops							$	1,200.00
Novelty activities		Prizes					$	1,000.00
Dog Tags							$	600.00
Postcards around America							$	750.00
Thumbprint Artist							$	350.00
Hi Striker							$	300.00
Dunk Tank							$	250.00
Speed Pitch							$	550.00
County Jail							$	400.00
Giant Slide							$	800.00
Obstacle Course							$	800.00
Pizza Chef							$	500.00
Moonwalk							$	200.00
Cow-milking Game							$	400.00
Uncle Sam Stiltwalking							$	450.00
Additional items		Photos					$	200.00
Staff supervision	8	Staff		$ 80.00			$	640.00
Planning fees							$	6,000.00
Flyers, notices/gift preparation							$	500.00
Total Outing Cost							$	**27,667.01**
T-shirts	198	Shirts		$ 5.75			$	1,138.50
Grand total with T-shirts							$	**28,805.51**
		Features		Venue A				
				Private facility				
				Indoor/outdoor setting: air-conditioning				
				Indoor toilets				
				Tasting available				
				Baseball/soccer field available				

Event info: Disc jockey and game show includes all props, DJ for entire event, and equipment necessary for game show.
Novelty prizes include giveaways for children's games and props for relays.
Decor includes balloons, tabletop items, props, and incidental raffle prizes for game show—pricing based on prior year's expenses.

	Venue B				Venue C		
	$ 28.95	pp	$ 3,618.75		$ 50.00	pp	$ 6,250.00
	$ 9.95	pp	$ 398.00		$ 12.00	pp	$ 480.00
			$ 4,016.75				**$ 6,730.00**
20	$ 1.50	each	$ 30.00		$ 2.50		$ 50.00
45	$ 2.00	each	$ 90.00		$ 2.50		$ 112.50
329	$ 3.00		$ 987.00		$ 3.50		$ 1,151.50
			$ 5,123.75				$ 8,044.00
		19%	$ 973.51			19%	$ 1,528.36
			$ 6,097.26				$ 9,572.36
		5%	$ 304.86			5%	$ 478.62
			$ 6,402.13				$ 10,050.98
	$ 30.00	3	$ 90.00				
					Signage		$ 350.00
	$ 75.00	5	$ 375.00		Mascot		$ 225.00
	$ 75.00	5	$ 375.00		Mascot		$ 225.00
	Beer/wine only		$ 75.00				$ 125.00
		n/a			n/a		
		n/a					$ 3,500.00
			$ 7,317.13				$ 14,475.98
			$ 2,700.00				$ 2,700.00
			$ 1,200.00				$ 1,200.00
			$ 1,000.00				$ 1,000.00
			$ 600.00				$ 600.00
			$ 750.00				$ 750.00
			$ 350.00				$ 350.00
			$ 300.00				$ 300.00
			$ 250.00				$ 250.00
			$ 550.00				$ 550.00
			$ 400.00				$ 400.00
			$ 800.00				$ 800.00
			$ 800.00				$ 800.00
			$ 500.00				$ 500.00
			$ 200.00				$ 200.00
			$ 400.00				$ 400.00
			$ 450.00				$ 450.00
			$ 200.00				$ 200.00
			$ 640.00				$ 640.00
			$ 6,000.00				$ 6,000.00
			$ 500.00				$ 500.00
			$ 25,907.13				**$ 33,065.98**
			$ 1,138.50				$ 1,138.50
			$ 27,045.63				**$ 34,204.48**

Venue B	Venue C
Open to public	Private
Outdoor only/tent with no sides	Under bleachers in protected area
Outdoor toilets	Indoor toilets
No tasting offered	Tasting available
No ball fields	Soccer available

A Billing Hint

As a consultant you will not need to purchase a great deal of inventory or have items in stock to show to clients. Any inventory can be purchased on a per-project basis with money you will receive *in advance* from the client. The best advice I can give is to set up your billing to reflect deposits and final payments prior to the date of each event. This will allow you to use your clients' funds for event purchases and vendor payments, instead of your own. You'll also eliminate nonpayment issues: no money, no event.

that they, too, need to price their services in a professional way. When the budget allows, showcase their best products and compensate them justly. Your valued vendors will understand the difficult task you have and appreciate you for using them for the variety of products or services they offer.

Budgeting

When putting together a budget for an event, you should take time to carefully estimate your costs in all areas. Step one is to start with the clients' budget. You will need to fully understand the clients' expectations for decor, cuisine, and entertainment, and counsel them on what can realistically be delivered. If their budget is $50,000, and the guest list is set at 500 people, you will be hard pressed to offer filet mignon for an entrée and still get paid as a planner. Before you spend time working up a detailed outline of services, you must educate them. Offer options for a variety of food, entertainment, and decor that will fit their budget and help them achieve their goals for the event.

In the worst case you may have to let a project go because there is no room for a planner's fee. Or you might opt to use your creative license and imagination to pare down costs yet still get the results the clients are looking for.

When creating a budget, I often have to present various options to help clients decide on the venue and other details that are right for them. Here is where the value of using a planner comes into play. They appreciate your expert advice and the time you've taken to compile the list of choices for their event. Once the research is done and the decisions are made, it's of course up to you to keep the project within budget.

Frequently Asked Questions

What is the best way to price my services?

That is the million-dollar question! It depends on the client, the budget, the scope of services, and your experience. Pricing also can be based on the advantage of working with a certain client, if there is additional work that can be secured by getting your foot in the door, or if there is a learning curve to the type of business that would warrant flexibility in pricing. Pricing can also be varied based on your current workload, the mix of events you may have and if you want to add a new "line" of services to your portfolio, the time of year that an event is requested, and if you really want the business. It is always best to look at the time you will be putting into the event and what other work you may lose if you commit to the event. Don't forget your life balance and if other areas of your life may suffer if you take an event that doesn't give you the remuneration that you need or deserve.

Should I treat nonprofit business differently? Can I make money working with this type of client?

Working with nonprofits can be advantageous in many ways. Not only can it provide repeat business (they may hold the same fund-raiser or conference each year), it can get you referrals, provide a philanthropic experience, allow you to advertise through sponsorship of events, and also provide an opportunity to use students, interns, or novice planners who will donate their time for a good cause. I typically will discount my fees for a not-for-profit client, but will show them my full fee structure, so they realize the value they are receiving.

Should I show my fee directly to the client, or should I bury it in the total costs of the event?

I like to present a line item for my services so that the client can clearly see the value of my work. I often will create a detailed task analysis showing the hours it will take for planning, which then will give me total hours and a total fee. Sometimes a commission or fee for securing sponsorship will allow for more flexibility for the client, and can offer more of an incentive, but is more risky.

Should I get payment in full before an event takes place?

If you can, it is an excellent way to keep your company in a positive cash-flow situation. It will also allow the client's check to clear your bank account before you have to issue checks to vendors. If you present your payment structure up front, when you are in the contract-signing phase, there will be no surprises for either you or the client. As long as you keep your budget up-to-date and get approval for any additions or changes, presenting the final bill to your client should be a positive experience. You will also be building good relationships with your vendors as you pay them in full and on a timely basis.

05

Marketing Your Services

To successfully start and grow an event planning business, you must have the magical mix of superior service and a strong customer base. You've already formalized your business identity and set up financial procedures; now you're ready to begin the search for a paying customer.

Specialist or Generalist? Defining Your Position

As a full-service event planner, you'll want to maintain a clear focus on what you do and how you execute the planning process. This will allow you to deliver concise information to potential clients. Some planners feel specialization allows them to focus their energies on one area. This could be with the type of planning you offer or the industry you target. Niche marketing, in the right industry or area, can position you as an expert and give you an edge by saturating one specific market. Others feel that by maintaining a broad scope of services, they are better poised to take advantage of changing business climates and industry highs and lows.

I have done both in my own career. In the 1990s my client portfolio included companies in the telecommunications industry as well as Internet companies. They were booming at the time and great sources of ongoing projects and referrals. Over the past few years, however, these clients have mysteriously disappeared from my schedule. The changing economy has forced me to redirect my energies and seek out other sources of corporate business. I've chosen to expand my services to include social events, an area that I hadn't developed in the past. I've now opened up my services to select wedding clients, high-end social events, and fund-raising events. While making a move to market to a

More on Image

It goes without saying that in developing your company image, you should carry your marketing plan through to your presentational plan as well. Attire, portfolio, and presentational material . . . all these should reflect the company image you have chosen. Think about the clothing you wear. Would a contemporary Armani suit over a sparkly top best reflect your style—or maybe a classic blazer or suit? If you're dealing with children's events, on the other hand, taking a more casual approach won't jeopardize your reputation or the impression you make with your clients. In any case, professional, organized, knowledgeable, and prepared should be the impression you leave after meeting with potential customers. This can also be reflected in your prompt follow-up, quick delivery of promised proposals, and timeliness at meetings.

new type of event client, I have stayed as close to my forte as possible, dealing with customers who are looking for a professional implementation of their event—a planner who is experienced in managing all aspects of the process, from creative development to contract management, professional execution, and the final stages of follow-up and evaluation.

Wouldn't it be nice if there were a crystal ball to tell you the future of event planning! Unfortunately, so many factors can affect why and who chooses to hold an event. My advice would be to find an area you enjoy and are naturally skilled at. Whether that means dealing with the concerns of a bride or responding to the empty look of a CEO who has no clue what she wants for her company awards dinner, target the clients you can most easily relate to and go for it.

Branding Your Company
The Defining Statement

Begin crafting your marketing materials with a defining sentence that will serve to brand your company identity going forward. You will use this as your marketing statement when you introduce yourself, meet potential clients, make presentations, or pitch your services to prospective customers during sales calls. *Fun, upscale, creative, classy, whimsical* . . . these descriptors and many more can be woven into your marketing statement.

Here are a few samples of defining statements:

- Hi, my name is Claire of A Wedding to Remember, and I specialize in weddings. I work with couples to make the details of the wedding flow smoothly and assist with the selection and management of the event vendors—florists, entertainment, linens, special transportation—to allow the bride and groom to create and enjoy memories of a lifetime!
- Hi, my company, Pizzazz Party Planning, creates events for children, including birthday parties, bar and bat mitzvahs, sweet sixteen parties, school fund-raising events, and children's fairs and festivals. We provide the specialty entertainment, inflatable games, festive novelties, and theme decor that

make each party truly unique for kids and families!

- Hello, I'm with Corporate Event Strategies. We handle the details of creating corporate events with our staff of event professionals through creative theme development and ongoing attention to detail. We produce internal events, marketing events, or training events at unique venues worldwide.

Creating Your Marketing Materials

Marketing materials are the tangible items that help a customer make the decision to hire you. Methods of delivery for this important information can range from Web sites, brochures, and postcards to PowerPoint and DVD presentations. In designing your marketing materials, you will want to be clear, succinct, colorful, and persuasive. Some clients will not be able to visualize your talents by reading a description. Photographs, sketches, or DVD clips can add a great deal to your marketing materials. Long-winded explanations will go unread, so short, powerful statements that show your style and value will be essential.

Web sites have become effective tools and cost relatively little in comparison to direct-mail pieces. They can reach a wide audience and allow you to update with ease. Not everyone is computer savvy, however, and some clients will want to "touch and feel" the service they will be buying. Brochures, personalized folders with inserts, or even postcards can capture the basics of your business and respond to these customers' needs. You may choose to develop a seasonal postcard

to send to a target audience, but in general mass mailings are costly and do not offer the return you will want from the investment made. Perhaps an advertisement in a specialty magazine will serve as a good marketing tool. Just remember to match the advertising vehicle with the customer base you're hoping to reach for maximum benefit.

Once you have your defining statement mapped out, you can use it to brand your marketing materials. At first you may choose or need to develop your own. This would be the most cost-effective way to get started. If you have photos or descriptions of events that you've produced, use these as a foundation to describe your services. If you're starting from scratch and have done any volunteer work, you may want to showcase your accomplishments for these projects. If you were in charge of the decorating committee and managed a staff to develop a theme and create the event decor, this could serve as an initial building block. Photos or words of praise can be included to show the success of the event. Be careful not to take credit for a project that you had only a small part in or were not directly involved with. If you helped another planner with an event, it would not be appropriate to describe that event in your portfolio or marketing material. If you feel you don't have enough experience to actually print a marketing piece, wait until you've done a few events on your own to create personalized materials.

To get started, you might address the elements that go into planning an event in a general way (just be ready to deliver these elements with an experienced support staff!). This would show your clients that you understand the process and can help them work through the many decisions required to create an event reflecting their goals, objectives, and personal tastes.

Here are some sample marketing pieces:

Affairs with Flair

Open your doors and allow us to set the table with fine linens upon which we place exquisite florals and gourmet cuisine prepared expressly for you and your guests.

At Affairs with Flair we offer event planning services with complete coordination of catering, linen, fine china, and serviceware rental; small musical ensemble entertainment; and floral and theme decor to complete the look of your special event! When you have a dream, but not the time to make it come true . . . let Affairs with Flair come to the rescue.

■ ■ ■

Party Pizzazz

Turning Forty, Getting Married, Celebrating an Anniversary . . . whatever the milestones in your life may be . . . let us help you celebrate with style! Party Pizzazz can assist with home parties or catered events at restaurants, hotels, or specialty venues. We complete the planning process with unique invitations, personalized decorations, full-service catering and beverage service, and entertainment to make your party the event of a lifetime!

■ ■ ■

What it Costs

Membership in a professional organization: $400 average per year, $30–$55 per monthly meeting

Ad in an industry publication: $50–$1,500

Article in an industry publication: free

Web site: $150–$2,500 (includes hosting fees and site development)

Television advertising: $50 (local)–$10,000 (national)

Ad production costs: $250–$2,500

Corporate Events Unlimited

At Corporate Events Unlimited, we specialize in the details of the event management process including site selection, vendor management, and execution of your internal or sales events. Partnering with you, we provide initial consultations, ongoing communications throughout the planning process, professional event execution, and complete evaluation to ensure that each event meets your company's goals and expectations. Leave the business of special event planning to the pros at Corporate Events Unlimited.

Developing a Marketing Plan
The Sales Challenge

It's not enough to have a formal event planning business . . . now you need clients. If you're lucky enough to have a few projects lined up, the pressure may be off for the time being. But one of the greatest challenges as a small-business owner is to be marketing your services while you're handling current planning tasks. You should try to set aside a certain percentage of your time to focus on securing new business. Try to answer inquiries when they come in. Turn proposals around on a timely basis in an attempt to have business in the pipeline. In a perfect world, when one project is complete, you'll have another waiting patiently to begin. Sounds good, but having the perfect balance of business is seldom a reality.

Either you're too busy to handle all the work coming your way, or you have time on your hands between projects wondering when the next event will arrive. Both situations come with solutions. If you're too busy working on projects to market on an ongoing basis, develop a mailer that you can send out monthly. Either write a newsletter or have someone do it for you. Perhaps a student intern could create a monthly flyer, which could be easily mailed to your target list of clients. Take time to get a Web site up and running. It will serve as an ongoing advertising vehicle. Keep it up to date with new photos, client testimonials, and event ideas. By staying in front of your existing clients and continually introducing yourself to potential customers, you keep the wheels of business turning. When an opportunity comes up, you'll be fresh in their minds.

Taking Care of Business!

Developing a solid system for categorizing leads is critical in the first stages of growing a business. Some possible lead management tools run from a basic Microsoft Office database such as Access

Getting Your Name Out There

Conventional methods:

- **Media.** Yellow pages, newspapers, local magazines, industry magazines.
- **Print.** Develop a print piece (like a postcard or brochure) to mail to potential customers.
- **Advertising.** Local, national, specialized.

Nonconventional methods:

- **Multimedia.** Develop a portfolio, a PowerPoint presentation, a video, or a CD to show potential clients.
- **Networking.**
- **Volunteerism.** Offer your services and/or advice.
- **Community.** Participate in career days and industry functions.

or Excel; others require a more professional management software system, such as ACT! by Symantec. There are many software tools on the market; ask at your local computer store for the latest and most popular software package, or do an Internet search to see what's new on the market. If you prefer jotting things down on paper, you might want to develop a file system using either file folders or index cards that contain key contact information and notes you make on an ongoing basis. After years of carrying a black book filled with business cards and addresses, I moved to a Palm Pilot and love the simplicity of finding everything in one place. While I still carry a notebook for jotting down ideas and daily lists, the important information gets logged into my Palm.

Put together your target "sales" list and mark your calendar with a plan of attack. Most sales are completed only after making many contacts. It takes persistence and a belief in your services and what you can bring to this client to make a lead turn into a sale. The sources of leads can vary from word-of-mouth referrals to lists that you purchase, leads from newspapers, and research you do on a particular market that you're targeting. However you develop your lead list, set up a system you can manage over time and set aside a portion of your planning week to take care of the business of selling!

Professional Involvement

Involvement in industry groups not only allows you to continue your own training and skills improvement, but also gives you an opportunity to build your vendor support as well as to form bonds with colleagues whom you can refer business to—or who could refer business back to you. A group of wedding planners in my area meets monthly for lunch to share vendor information, solutions to planning problems, and new wedding ideas or products they have discovered. They give each other "the scoop" on who's delivering the best or worst in vendor services. In a friendly way these competitors work together to stay on top of their game.

Attending monthly meetings of industry organizations can put your face and business on the map. It takes perseverance and dedication to carve an evening or two a month into your busy schedule to market yourself and your services. When my children were small, it was very difficult—if not

Sources of Leads

- **Professional organizations.** Serving on committees gives you great exposure. Networking at monthly meetings also can help develop contacts.
- **Chamber of commerce directories.** As a member of a chamber or business association, you have access to information on incoming groups and activities.
- **Newspaper want ad sections.** Look for event-related needs.
- **Newspaper articles.** Look for companies launching products, holding meetings, or expanding.
- **Newspaper social pages.** Look for leads on engagements, fund-raisers, or annual events.
- **Specialty magazines.** Business journals, meeting or incentive magazines, and bridal or corporate journals can give you advertising opportunities as well as names of vendors to contact.
- **Vendors.** All vendors have access to event clients who may need additional services.
- **Past clients.** Satisfied customers can provide you with referrals to other events.
- **Colleagues.** Event associates can refer business that they cannot or do not handle.

impossible. Between the travel obligations for my clients and the family extracurricular commitments, I just wasn't able to attend a majority of these meetings. Over time, though, I made a commitment to become active in a leadership role in my local International Special Events Society

(ISES) chapter. And by doing so, I've made business contacts and professional friendships that I couldn't live without!

Consider joining allied associations such as the National Association of Catering Executives (NACE), Meeting Professionals International (MPI), or the Professional Convention Management Association (PCMA). It can be time-consuming to attend meetings, but it's also a great way to get to know colleagues who could refer business to you. People like to do business with friends, and networking events are a great way get exposure.

At the very least you should become an ISES member. It's a professional investment well worth making. The International Special Events Society is the organization that defines and refines the event industry. When you become a member, you have the option of joining a local chapter. Once you join, offer to sit on a committee—or better yet, begin to familiarize yourself enough with the chapter to chair a committee. In any of the related hospitality organizations, the best way to reap benefits is to become active. Everyone will know who you are. And when someone is looking for a planner, your name will be the first to come up.

Below you'll find the Web sites of the hospitality and event industry's key organizations. Some of these sites also list other related professional organizations. Check appendix B for a complete list of hospitality-related organizations and their contact information.

- International Special Events Society (ISES): www.ises.com
- National Association of Catering Executives (NACE): www.nace.net
- Meeting Professionals International (MPI): www.mpiweb.org
- Professional Convention Management Association (PCMA): www.pcma.org

Network

Networking is a great marketing tool that allows you to sell your services in a more personalized way. You can make an instant impression on a possible client—and vice versa: You can assess a prospect's sales potential quickly and interactively. Face-to-face contact also allows you to ask for a commitment for a follow-up meeting—even to set up a day and time.

Networking can occur at professional meetings, social or civic gatherings, or with community groups. Check your local papers for lunch-hour networking groups. Inquire as to the types of companies that are currently members. Assess the value of joining before spending any money on dues. If members could potentially use your services or refer you business, it's worth at least trying out a meeting or two. Some groups have limits as to how many meetings you can attend before committing to membership. In any case decide on how much time you have to give to this piece of your marketing strategy, and choose the groups that best meet your needs.

For me the broader industry groups like ISES and MPI as well as membership in my local convention and visitor bureau offered me a broad range of corporate and social opportunities. The local CVB gave me access to incoming groups and

Networking Dos & Don'ts

Do . . .

- Arrive early.
- Bring plenty of business cards and a pen.
- Jot down information on a card about each person you speak to and when you'll follow up.
- Be ready—have a one- or two-sentence description of what you do.
- Gather more than you give.
- Make a good impression.

Don't . . .

- Try to juggle a plate of hors d'oeuvres and a drink while you try to shake a new acquaintance's hand.
- Stick only with people you know.
- Spend more than three to five minutes with each person.
- Oversell. Instead, plan a follow-up meeting at which you can give your full sales presentation.

and make plans for follow-up. Check the sidebar for some pointers to get you off to the right start.

Places to Network

Networking opportunities can be found in industry meetings, at locally sponsored events, and even at social gatherings. All of these offer an opportunity to tell your story and gather information.

- **Hotels.** Quite often people start their event planning process with the place where they'd like to hold the event. Hotel professionals may be able to offer venue and catering services, but not extended event services such as entertainment, decor, invitations, lighting, or party favors. By coming up with a list of possible hotels that attract the type of clients you'd like to work with, you may be bringing a service to the hotel as well as its customers. Positioning yourself as a "preferred vendor" or "strategic partner," you can add value to what the hotel can offer while expanding your business at the same time.
- **Specialty venues** such as ballrooms, meeting halls, museums, aquariums, and restaurants can offer the same opportunities as hotels. Their clients often need the support services of an event planner, and by becoming a resource to the venue you expand your opportunities.
- **Vendors** can be a major source of new business. Once you establish yourself with a group of colleagues, it's as if you've expanded your own sales force. A caterer may have a client who's looking for invitations, for instance; a tent rental company that's exclusive to a country

leads on clients that would need planning services for trade-show-related events. If your target market is social business, a wedding or catering organization might afford stronger leads. If you're targeting a certain geographic area, a local business networking group might be the right fit.

The best way to approach networking is to go in with a plan. This isn't a time for free food and wine—it's a chance to gather leads, take notes, club may be asked to recommend a planner. Vendors have become a major source of referrals for my business over the years. Treat your vendors well by thanking them for their quality work and products.

More Ways to Gain Exposure for You and Your Company

- **Volunteer.** Remember, "What goes around, comes around." Donate a portion of your time. Stand out from the crowd . . . raise your hand . . . don't wait to be asked. Volunteer opportunities abound, from fund-raising events to industry or meeting committees. By giving your time, energy, and creative ideas for all to see, you create visibility and recognition for yourself.

- **Educate yourself.** Take courses on event-related subjects at local colleges or universities. Many schools are adding event-related courses to their continuing education programs. Most cities offer seminars or conferences for the hospitality, meeting, and event industries. These are great places to meet colleagues and pick up ideas. Whether the courses cover professional skill building, event design and trends, or business management tools, they'll add to the knowledge you need to grow and manage your business. Some courses provided by the International Special Events Society can provide the basic foundation for achieving your Certified Special Events Professional designation. All of these educational opportunities add to your value, give you additional contacts, and let you have more to talk about when in a meeting with a client or following up with a prospect.

(See chapter 13 and the appendices for a full discussion.)

- **Be a leader.** Share your expertise with those in your field or industry, in your community, or in other industries. Each year I participate in career day at our local middle school. I talk with the kids about my career and take a group of students with me for "a day in the life of an event planner." Depending on the mix of students, I try to schedule a visit to the site where an upcoming event will be held. I've taken the kids to a sports stadium that was being prepared for a company outing. In past years the field trip has included a visit to a design center for theme materials, and lunch and discussion with a chef regarding the menu for an upcoming event. I discuss theme and giveaway ideas with the students, and even do some pre-event shopping when possible. These students get not only a behind-the-scenes view of a special venue, but also a glimpse at what goes on when an event is planned. They also have parents whose employers might someday need event services—or who may need help with a particular celebration themselves.

- **Be seen.** Write articles for local and industry magazines sharing your experiences. If there are publications that address event topics, perhaps you can offer insight on a venue you've used, ideas on current themes or decor trends, or challenges that your customers may face and how to address them. Over the years I've made contact with several event-related magazines and had articles published in them. I let my colleagues know that I like to write, and they refer me on as well. The key to getting new business with this is to get your event-related articles into magazines in other industries— say, journals in the pharmaceutical, meeting management, or trade show fields. Find out who to contact and offer to share your expertise on event topics. When these magazines hit the hands of the executives who need event services . . . you're the expert.

- **And be heard.** Offer to speak at local or national events within or outside your industry, as well as at colleges, local schools, and public or charity events. This will help you define your skills and clarify your game plan.

Everything starts with a sale. Remember, somewhere out there, someone is looking for you and needs your services. You just have to make the connection. If you've honed your skills and have an excellent service to offer, you *will* make it happen. Believe in yourself, and approach the task of marketing your services with determination and a positive attitude.

As you progress through the phases of getting your business up and running, be aware that you'll be constantly defining and refining your skills. Your marketing efforts should thus let customers know about the changes you're making to add value to their event experiences. Take a long hard look at your skills and what you do best, and present them in the best light possible. Be visible in your industry, among your peers and competitors and (especially) potential clients. Take every opportunity to spread the word that you are an event planner who will make a difference.

Frequently Asked Questions

Should I specialize or generalize?

It depends on your skills and interests. I have developed a broad scope of services for my company, which has allowed me to ride through economic and seasonal changes. It also provides variety in events and clients and keeps me fresh with my ideas and concepts. The downside of variety is being diluted in your approach or confusing to clients that really want that "wedding planner" or "meeting planner." I have tried to keep my Web site organized and easy to search for clients that only want to see my new social events or learn more about nonprofit work I am doing. If you are passionate about weddings, be a wedding planner. If you love to work with kids, be the best children's party planner around. Don't be afraid to throw all your event eggs in one basket. But if you like variety, make sure you are up on the differences between event markets and can switch hats easily.

Do I need to take advertisements out in local papers?

It's not a bad idea to advertise if you know that the ad will reach the people who will buy your services. There are other ways to get your name out there, including sponsorship, trade show attendance, networking, and volunteering in your community. Word of mouth goes a long way in passing your name to the right potential client. Build your reputation event by event by delivering the kind of service you are proud of. Don't underestimate nontraditional ways of advertising. All of these marketing tactics can help get your name out to those who may need your services.

Should I join a professional organization?

Joining a professional group will benefit you through networking with vendors, potential clients, and potential staff; provide education and resource information; and give you a chance to perfect your skills while serving as a leader in the industry. There are plenty of opportunities to assist with monthly meetings and industry events and try your event skills out as a volunteer. You will also develop a reputation in the industry and make contacts that can generate business. Don't expect to get a lead at every meeting or justify your expenses at a conference with direct business. Sometimes it takes months or years for your name to be recognized and for business to come your way. But in the meantime, you build your event skills and people skills by being active in the industry.

06

Developing a Team

All businesses are built upon layers of skills. While some entrepreneurs have a broad range of skills to offer, most companies are made of a palette of support personnel. Different staff members will fulfill administrative, customer service, and project management duties. In the field of event planning, the owner of the business is typically the one with the creative and entrepreneurial spirit. Unfortunately, to run a business successfully, this often just isn't enough; you must balance the skills you do have with the ones you don't. In other words, even if you're not good at—or happy about—financial planning, record keeping, and risk analysis tasks, they still need to be part of your daily and monthly routine. Take an honest look at your skill set, and be prepared to complement your strengths with outside support for your weaknesses.

Support, Part I: Vendors

To plan and execute your first event, you'll need support. As you grow, your support team will grow with you as well. For your first event you may want to do most of the decor yourself or enlist some volunteers to help with setup or teardown. Soon, however, you won't have time to inflate all the balloons (for instance), and you'll look for a pro who can handle this important decor element. I enlisted Christine Bernstein of Balloon City of Boston for a corporate anniversary event many years ago. While I don't use balloons in every event, Bernstein keeps me up on new techniques and decorating ideas incorporating balloons to keep me on the edge of my game. The same goes with my favorite caterers or linen rental companies. There's no way I could keep up on all

What Skills Do You Need?

Running a successful event planning business involves a sweeping range of skills:

- **Administrative skills.** Tracking and analyzing your finances.
- **Marketing skills.** Keeping your company in the public eye.
- **Sales skills.** Touting yourself and closing the deal.
- **People skills.** Balancing conflicting needs while making everyone happy.
- **Creative skills.** Making each event an artful, memorable experience.
- **Execution skills.** Preparing seventeen dozen gourmet canapés, inflating fourteen dozen ballons, repairing a flickering spotlight, interviewing seven jazz bands, decorating a six-layer cake, arranging several thousand dollars' worth of flowers, finalizing camera angles with a videographer, designing invitations that are traditional—yet trendy—and setting up sixteen portable toilets.
- **Project management skills.** Overseeing all of the above at the same time . . . well.

If you think you might be lacking in some of these areas—read on.

Here's a sampling of some of the vendors you might want to turn to:

- Caterer
- Florist
- Invitation designer
- Photographer
- Videographer
- Rental company
- Balloon artist
- Makeup artist
- DJ
- Caricaturist
- Entertainment agency
- Casino table provider
- Fabric supply company
- Magician
- Prop company
- Tent company
- Venues: casino, hotel, ballroom, country club
- Transportation: bus, limo, etc.
- Decor provider
- Staffing company
- Lighting company
- Electrical provider
- . . . and many others

the latest designs and techniques in every discipline, so I look to experts help me to offer the latest and greatest to my clients. By pulling together the right team, your events can meet or exceed your expectations time after time.

These are the pros you'll call on for linens, rentals, florals, and photography . . . the ones who'll set up or tear down your event . . . the people who will meticulously put together your giveaway bags or hand-tie the wedding invitations that you create. This "human tool kit" is the final layer of the preparations you'll make for starting your event planning business. You may not need every type of vendor for every event you plan, of course. Still, it's never too soon to start pulling together your list. Be sure to keep adding to it as you gather experience and references.

How do you find good vendors? Everywhere and anywhere. Here are a few places to start:

- Industry groups (events, meetings, conferences)
- Local business networking groups and chambers of commerce
- Referrals from other planners
- Referrals from venues (hotels, country clubs, event facilities)
- Referrals from industry contacts who have exposure to a variety of services
- Professional trade shows and conferences
- Trade magazines
- Colleges or universities

Evaluating Vendors

How do you know if a particular vendor is a good match for your company? Here are some things to look for:

- Service specifics
- Professional training
- Experience
- Customer base
- Years in business
- Communication skills
- Attention to detail
- Flexibility
- Professionalism

Be sure to file every lead you come across in an organized way for easy retrieval when you need it. On page 68 there is a sample form you might use to record vendor information for your files.

I receive many brochures and other pieces from suppliers and vendors, which I file away until the right project calls for a certain specialized service or product. You may not need a juggler, circus group, or magician for every event, but if the call comes in, you'll want to have a reference number on hand.

Support, Part II: Staffing

You may go into your business as the chief cook and bottle washer, but it won't be long before you realize you can't do it all. It may be difficult to have on hold a team ready and waiting to help you put together invitations, dress tables with linens, or park cars, but these are the very real nuts and bolts of the event business. Where can you turn to get support in delivering the quality you boast of?

Students

Not a week goes by that I don't receive an e-mail from a college student looking for advice and experience. Due to the nature of the business, it is often feasible to use these ambitious young enthusiasts for weekend or evening events. It may be worthwhile to meet with them, do some preliminary screening, and compile a list to use for future projects.

Some schools have work-study programs that provide paid or unpaid job experience. Contact

Vendor Information Sheet

Name: _____

Address: _____

_____

_____

Phone: _____ Fax: _____

E-mail: _____

Years in business: _____

Current clients: _____

_____

_____

Types of business services: _____

_____

_____

Types of events services: _____

_____

_____

Specialties: _____

_____

_____

Pricing: _____

_____

_____

Payment structure (COD, credit card, purchase order, thirty-day invoice): _____

_____

Referral letters: _____

_____

_____

_____

the career placement or financial aid office at institutions in your vicinity to sign up for eligible students.

Relatives and Friends

Many start-up entrepreneurs enlist family members in the company's early stages. I was lucky enough to work side by side with my dad in his moving and storage business from the time I was in high school. It offered me great training in business and served as the foundation for my future event business. Now my daughters and son work with me at my events, and they often bring several of their friends to staff the kids' area at company outings or help with setup and teardown. You, too, may have relatives or friends who can offer expertise and trustworthy support.

War Stories: Helper Horror

For a corporate event I hired some extra staff to assist with setup. Since these were older folks, I didn't go over event etiquette during my pre-event briefing. During the event, however, one woman proceeded to behave like a guest—helping herself to the open bar and food and circulating with the attendees. I gently guided her back to her post, but the incident was certainly a poor reflection on my company. Remember to hold your staff accountable for their behavior, and be clear about your expectations up front before the party begins.

Colleagues

Once you begin publicizing your new business, you'll run across innumerable people who share your passion for the events industry. Keep in contact with them. They can be excellent referral sources for business you cannot handle (and of course they might pass business on to you). You may be able to partner up with your peers on a project that's beyond your scope at a given time, or use them to supplement your resource team. There's nothing better than having a staff familiar with the event process who'll approach it in the same professional way you do.

Don't forget to repay the favor by helping out your colleagues when they need you, too!

Nonworking Professionals

Nicole Samolis of The Events Company from Syracuse, New York, uses a group of at-home moms as her team. She selects women in her community who are trustworthy, capable, and dependable to arrive for early setup and to return to the events for teardown at the end of the night. She no longer has to personally attend each event from start to finish, opening her schedule up for more important leadership duties. And her team members have a part-time job that's flexible, fun, and easy to fit into their lives.

Professional Organizations

The beauty of belonging to a professional organization like the International Special Events Society is how easily it puts you into contact with a network of professionals. Whether your events

Staffing Needs

What kinds of needs should you look to your staff to fill? Here are some functions to think about:

Event Preparation:

- Assembling invitations, gift or goodie bags, favors, name badges, briefing booklets, and programs
- Decor production, including purchasing, ordering, assembling, constructing, sewing, painting, and decorating specialized decor you select for your events

Catering:

Most of the time, the caterers you hire will provide the support they need, but make sure they cover all the bases:

- Food and beverage preparation and delivery
- Serviceware rental and setup, including china, glassware, utensils, napkin folding
- Tray decorations for passed hors d'oeuvres
- Buffet treatments, including all serviceware and utensils
- Cleanup and refuse removal

Decor and Event Execution:

Some vendors will handle production specialties, such as tenting, lighting, and audio-visual or power service. But there are some functions that you'll handle through your own staffing:

- Linen placement
- Floral placement
- Tent accessories, such as light strings, vines, florals, and fabric draping
- Room decor, including buffets, walls, ceilings, dining tables, and specialty stations such as gift tables, sign-in areas, and ceremony basics (runners, aisle markers, arbors)
- Teardown and removal

Event Staffing:

You may prefer to select professionals to handle such tasks as security or parking, or you might choose to support the venue's offerings with additional staffing:

Registration	Gift dissemination	Valet
Directing guests	Help desk	Coat check
Instant photographers	Security	Cleanup

are in your local area or produced around the world, trusted colleagues are ready and waiting for your call. Don't be afraid to perform a quick check of references to get an overview of people's skills and make sure they match your needs.

Trained Staffing Agencies

Staffing agencies can provide insured, bonded professionals to provide services from wait staff and food preparers to bartending services. In my area, for example, Betsy Duffy of House Helpers provides catering staff for an array of intimate dinner engagements and parties including full kosher meals. And the Pour People in nearby Providence, Rhode Island, handle bar service with staff who are TIPS certified, guaranteeing their completion of a certification program that includes all bonding procedures and training, and emphasizes responsible alcoholic beverage service. They provide all drink-related products and bring out the latest in mixers, colored sugars, and the like.

The best place to find good sources for temporary help is to ask colleagues or friends for referrals. If you aren't coming up with any leads, you can always check your local or regional yellow pages under employment agencies, staffing services, employment contractors, or temporary help. Working through agencies can provide you with insured and bonded staff but will be more costly. Refine your search to your specific need such as security, food service, catering staff, and valet services when searching the Web or your local yellow pages.

Don't fall into the trap of paying a worker as a subcontractor to avoid workers' compensation

What it Costs

Office Assistant: $0 (intern) to $25 per hour (to complete proposals, input data, or do market research)

Event Assistants: $0 (intern) to $50 (depending if design or preparation work is required and on their experience level)

Event Manager: $25–$50 per hour. It can be difficult to get an event manager on a per-project basis, so it may be worth compensating them to ensure they will be available when events arise. If you find someone who works well and you are keeping them busy, it may be time to hire your first employee!

and payroll taxes and the other commitments that go with hiring an employee. If you control not only what a worker does but how it is to be done, that worker is likely an employee, and you can be held liable for failing to carry workers' compensation insurance or to pay payroll taxes.

You may reach a point where it makes sense to hire someone either full or part time. Perhaps you find someone who can handle administrative duties, works well on site at events, learns quickly, works efficiently, and shares the same passion for events as you do. Making the commitment to hire an employee increases your financial responsibility (you will have a weekly commitment to pay your new employee), record keeping (you must take proper deductions for tax purposes and file appropriately), legal and risk exposure (you are legally responsible for employees' actions while

Subcontractor vs. Employee

Subcontractors

Pros:

- You don't undertake any long-term financial responsibility.
- You don't have to pay employment taxes or workers' compensation insurance.
- You don't have to provide employee benefits such as health insurance, vacations, holidays, and sick days.
- You can select the best candidate with the best skill set for each project.

Cons:

- It may be difficult to find consistent help.
- The best help may not be available when you need them.
- More effort must be made in training as new staff are used.

Employees

Pros:

- You can train employees to maximize their performance in your business culture.
- You can delegate more tasks to your employees to allow for more effective use of your own time (management, marketing, and so on).

Cons:

- You must have enough business to keep them busy.
- Record keeping for payroll and employer tax returns becomes more complicated.
- You have more responsibility for supervision.
- You're directly liable for employees' acts or omissions.

they are representing you and your company). Growth is a great thing, but it does have its fair share of complications and responsibilities. Plan for the changes you want to make by having a strong book of business in the pipeline and by carefully screening your contract staff.

Working with Your Support Staff
Compensating Your Vendors

For the most part many vendors on your list can provide you with lists of their services and prices. Most will also offer a range of prices to respond to a variety of customer needs. This way, once you find a reliable rental or linen company, you simply select from its options and styles to fit your clients' budget.

Some vendors will have sample books, catalogs, or price sheets for you to examine; look for these among linen companies, tableware rental companies, and invitation designers. On the other hand production or lighting companies whose services include extensive setup and labor charges tend to quote each project individually. Many factors can affect the price they'll quote you, including the location of the event, the time of year or day the event is being held, setup and teardown requirements, and how their services will be used in the overall event process.

You should be able to get a range of pricing quotes—prices for everything from single appointments to comprehensive services, and from high to medium and low budgets. Even so, it's always wise to include these types of vendors in your bidding process. They may also have suggestions to trim your budget or boost your event's thematic flair.

Compensating Your Staff

You will want to build a reliable and motivated team to assist you during the many facets of the event process. You should pay them a fair wage while providing a stimulating and educational environment in the midst of the long hours and sometimes stressful moments of executing an event. Some of your staff might be young teens assisting with family events or working behind the scenes. Others might be seasoned hospitality pros looking to brush up on their planning skills and earn some extra money on the side. Each will be treated differently. Their wages will be based on a combination of their experience and the type of work they're doing, while keeping in mind what your event budget will bear. I always figure in extra costs for staffing my events. It also helps to tip your support team based on the hours they work and their overall effort and willingness to be at your beck and call. Your main goal will be to grow a team that you can rely on and who'll be there for you when you need them, so it's best to make the job worth their while!

Job Requirements and Expectations

It's always a good idea to go over all of your expectations with each vendor and staff member in advance. This can be accomplished during an initial meeting and repeated at the pre-event walk-through. Duties can change from job to job, and client to client, so make a thorough review of your needs in writing prior to each event. The

When to Bring in the Pros

When you realize the scope of writing your contracts or reviewing your insurance programs is beyond your ability to address prudently, it's time to bring in the pros. You work hard to convince others of the benefits of hiring an event specialist—and the same goes for the specialists who can help you in your business. If you select wisely, they are worth every cent you pay them.

Here are some of the professionals you might consult in the course of doing business:

- Accountant
- Lawyer
- Communications specialist
- Computer professional
- Insurance agent
- Bookkeeper

When looking for professional support, select people who are versed in your business or at least in small home-based businesses. They should be familiar with the unique qualities of special events, the liabilities you are exposed to, your cash-flow patterns, and the way you use technology. They should not only respond to your questions but be proactive about advising you of current changes, trends, techniques, or opportunities.

Try to engage these experts on a specified or as-needed basis. You will not need an accountant to meet with you monthly, but you may need a bookkeeper each month and your accountant semiannually to support your ongoing record keeping. The same holds true for your legal counsel. If you can commit to a flat fee for a specified number of calls or consulting appointments, you can be more relaxed about calling your attorney when something doesn't look right in a contract or you are concerned over a liability issue. Look for someone who appears interested in your business, is available for you in small increments of time, and doesn't mind that you're not a big-name client.

Responsibility Chart

Well before your event, spell out who is responsible for each of the following:

- Rental setup, teardown, and pickup
- Permits and licenses
- Power limitations or enhancements
- Safety measures
- Security
- Food requirements for vendors and staff

overall production schedule you create will drive most of the specific timing—arrival, setup schedule, and post-event pickup. You might want to go even further, however, spelling out such details as who will set up the tables once they're delivered, and who will set the linens out and collect them at the end of the event. All of this should be confirmed prior to signing contracts and placing final orders. Remember, time is money. If you'll be paying your staff to perform duties that relate to vendor rentals, you should be compensated for it. You may have to include additional fees for this work, so consider these issues before you submit your final proposal to your client.

Evaluations

Just as important as thanking people for a job well done is letting them know when they haven't met your expectations. Sometimes the problem can be due to poor communication up front. Perhaps you didn't adequately stress the importance of lighting in the catering tent or failed to mention that you'd need wheelchair access for guests. Even if you perform a pre-event walk-through, don't take for granted that vendors and staff will know what you want. Write it down. Insert it in a contract. Discuss any special needs you may have well in advance of the event.

Once the event is over, it's critical to hold a discussion with each vendor and staffer. Review what worked, what didn't, and what could be changed to improve the process next time. If done in a constructive way, this conversation can offer encouragement and demonstrate that you're interested enough in the relationship to work on improving it and create an even better event the next time around.

Once you've assembled the various support systems, you can begin to envision your company as an entity—an orchestra, if you will. You are the conductor of this fabulous ensemble, which sometimes performs classical music, sometimes modern, and sometimes rock! As the conductor, you're in charge of keeping the parts together and creating an end result that leaves your audience in awe. It's a sizable task but, with the right team, it's also rewarding for everyone involved.

Frequently Asked Questions

How can I make sure my vendors and contract labor will provide the kind of service I really want?

Make sure you clearly outline your expectations to all parties involved. It is a good idea to issue a vendor contract and even provide your contract labor with an agreement formalizing your expectations and payment policies. As these folks are not employees, your requirements for insurances, taxes, and payments may be different for each person and may vary from event to event. You should review your event in full: the client, the venue, the theme, and most important your production schedule and timeline. Even if a client has a short production schedule and there are last-minute decisions being made, make sure you update all parties involved. It's always a good idea to have a pre-event meeting, even if it is only hours before the event to identify the key people and any nuances that you want everyone to be aware of. This will ensure that the event has your stamp of approval on it!

I need quite a few extra hands for an upcoming fund-raiser, but I don't have the money in the budget for staffing. How can I make things happen without working 24/7 the week before the event?

Volunteers can be a great way to staff events if you find the right people. Local colleges or universities can be a great source of interns, many of whom may have experience already or be in hospitality or event-related degree programs. Some will require a minimum number of hours; others will allow students to sign up directly with you when opportunities arise. You may have a post-event evaluation to complete, but using students can be an inexpensive way to solve staffing problems and give you a chance to test a potential employee out before you make the plunge.

How can I build a list of good vendors to use?

Most of the time, you can get referrals from other event planners on who they use for specific services. It's best to ask at industry meetings and begin forming a list before you need them. Visit their offices, check out their portfolios, and get references from satisfied clients or planners. Don't wait until you absolutely need a service to begin looking; you'll be left scrambling and may have to use someone who is not the best fit for your event.

Should I plan to take all the labor costs out of my commission or fee?

I typically will add a line item to reflect labor on events. This may include the cost of set-up, teardown, table dressing/setting and chair tying, invitation or goodie bag assembly. These are all items that also can be reflected in the cost of the service. Some linen

Frequently Asked Questions (continued)

companies will ship you the linens and you are responsible for setting them up. The same holds true with rentals of tables and chairs. You will be left with racks of chairs, bins of plates, and unfolded napkins to set up and fold yourself if you don't plan ahead. You can group the labor costs into the item, but don't forget to add these on to the material costs before inputting it in as a line item for your client's budget.

07

Legal and Ethical Issues

As you'll learn very quickly in the event planning business, it's not enough to know the tricks of the trade in decor, florals, or production techniques; you must also take a hard look at the elements of each event that could open you up to liability, and learn how to minimize your risk and increase the safety of your clients and event attendees. While you should be aware of any changing regulations that affect the event industry, staying abreast of changing laws and requirements is best left for the professionals in the fields of law, management, and insurance. For this reason I suggest selecting an attorney who can guide you through the important task of creating basic contracts and updating these on a per-event basis as needed. Establishing a business relationship with an attorney is a prudent step to take for the safety and security of your business as well as the events you produce and the guests that attend them.

Liability

According to attorney James N. Decoulos of Decoulos Law in Peabody, Massachusetts, who specializes in legal and insurance issues for event professionals, you must be aware of liability throughout every phase of the event planning process. Events are often emotionally charged, and they may contain elements of surprise that could result in disaster if not planned for appropriately. As you create dynamic environments with decor, offer food prepared off site, and select artists and entertainers who bring their own set of performance issues and dangers, you may become liable for damages sustained by vendors, venues, and

War Stories: Sick and Sicker

Mike Gallant of Perfect Parties was providing musical entertainment at a wedding when he received word that an elderly guest had fainted on the dance floor. Trained in CPR, Gallant knew what to do, but he quickly realized that the situation was serious. He requested immediate medical attention—and the townwide siren sounded to notify EMTs. The raid signal, in addition to the very ill woman lying prone on the dance floor, panicked everyone in the room, and they began fainting and vomiting. By the time the victim was removed by stretcher to the hospital, at least twenty more partygoers had taken ill. To avoid continued mass hysteria, Gallant requested the use of an adjacent empty ballroom to move people away from the chaos.

The moral of the story? Think through an evacuation and safety plan before you start any event and share it with everyone involved.

Decoulos highlights the importance of liability issues by noting that failing to cope with them can lead to business failure and even personal financial ruin. Here are some of his tips for responding to the tremendously complex issues surrounding event liability:

- Learn to understand what in the course of conducting an event represents exposure to liability and how best to minimize it.
- Embrace liability as an ally. Liability is at once a sword and a shield. Use your contracts both to protect yourself and to bind clients.
- Don't overlook details about the fundamental business relationship between you and your clients, especially at the proposal phase. This is particularly so for last-minute bookings, which you may take on hoping to impress a client and gain repeat business. In the flurry of work such bookings involve, it's easy to neglect even issues as obvious as when and how you'll be paid.
- A contract is not fully formed simply with agreement upon a price. In fact, a price isn't even required for a contract to be considered in effect. What is necessary is enough detail to create a binding relationship between you and your clients. (See the "Contracts" section on page 79 for more information.)
- Be succinct and specific. There's a fine art to reducing into writing all the essential details about what you will and won't provide—and this is an art worth cultivating. Does obtaining an event license mean paying for the licensing fee or other costs such as bonding or producing a floor plan? Often a licensing authority will

attendees at your events. Issues can range from an injured guest to food poisoning, falling props, and misfired pyrotechnics. While most of these unplanned occurrences aren't necessarily the fault of the event planner, it's critical that you show due diligence, taking all necessary precautions to avoid problems. These include thoroughly researching the qualifications, experience, and reputations of everyone you deal with. More potential issues that could involve liability include the consulting contract, site selection, food and beverage service, entertainment, subcontracts, security, and licensing.

require special police and fire details at additional cost. When such requirements are discovered, and the additional expense becomes an adjustment of the contract price, immediate written notification must be made to (and an acknowledgment received from) the client.

- Short simple letters written during the progress of work function well, even if only to document the efforts that are being made to fulfill the contract. If you fail to do so, you may well be forced to absorb additional expenses from your profit. In the case of the event licenses mentioned above, failure to discover the licensing requirement in the first instance may subject you and your clients to fines, cease-and-desist orders, or both. It is reasonably unlikely that all such details will be available at the contract formation stage. Therefore provisions should be made for modifying the basic contract in the course of performance.

- Carefully review your client engagement letter. It should contain essential terms such as the date of contract, date of performance, contract amount, deposit, progress and final payments, time and manner of payment, and specification of all goods and services to be provided, as well as any items unique to the special event. If a guarantee is offered, it should be worded to an objective standard. Use disclaimers to detail what isn't guaranteed—for example, the weather and a good turnout.

Contracts

The safest and most responsible way to approach any business transaction is to clearly outline

War Stories: Crowd Control

If you deal with large public events, be prepared for misconduct and disorderly behavior. Even if liquor isn't available at a particular event, guests could arrive intoxicated. The owner of a local inflatables company shared with me his commitment to putting safety first. He and his staff must often make the call whether unruly guests should be allowed to partake in the fun. Saying no could result in a very angry patron; saying yes can be even riskier. Have enforcements ready, beyond the scope of your staff, to make sure things stay calm. If problems seem possible, don't hesitate to hire a private security firm or request a police detail.

what you will do and for what price. Rather than approaching contracting as something that makes the event process more cumbersome, approach it as protection for your company and your client. Formalizing your relationship will also help you avoid any misunderstandings.

You may know as an experienced planner that you'll perform certain duties during the event process, but your inexperienced clients may not have a clue. It's thus up to you to educate them so that the process is successful from start to finish. Following is a rough outline of a typical consulting agreement that I use—first an overview, then a more detailed description of its specific elements. I strongly suggest that you consult with an attorney, preferably one who specializes in event management, who can draft a contract that contains all the elements necessary to adhere to your own state and city laws.

Contract Essentials: An Overview

- Duties
- Payment
- Payment obligation and consequences
- Additional information
- Interpretation
- Cooperation
- Change orders
- Important dates
- Delays and extensions
- Inspections and approvals
- Termination
- Abandonment
- Payment of fees and permits
- Deviation from laws and regulations
- Completion of event
- Indemnity agreement
- Applicable law
- Agreement to perform
- Witness and signature line

Duties

In this paragraph you clearly identify the parties involved and the parameters of the event. Then list each specific category of items and services you'll be responsible for providing (the more detail, the better). These categories might include event preplanning and preparation, production scheduling, vendor selection and management, theme development, budgeting, promotion and marketing of the event, production of gift items, coordination of event details, on-site implementation, support and staffing, and evaluation. You can also break each of these down into sublists. For example, the *vendor selection and management* category might detail catering, rentals, linens, lighting, photography, decor, and transportation. The documents you'll continue to create during the planning process itself (production schedules, timelines, and so forth) will likely cover each of these entries in even further detail—but do be sure that the contract includes a thorough listing of categories.

Payment

Here you'll identify the payment agreed upon and the payment schedule. You might break this down into two or more payments based on the size and scope of the project. Also list any expenses that you expect to be reimbursed for. These might include office or travel expenses unique to the project. It would be appropriate to promise detailed lists of expenses and statement summaries to support the cost of the event as the event progresses. You should also identify your payment policy. This includes specifically when you expect advance payments and when the clients must pay based on any bills you present.

Payment Obligation and Consequences

Just as you're committing to deliver a service, you're also asking that your clients commit to compensating you for your time. In this area you would identify consequences of nonpayment, which could include termination or cancellation of contract, as well as collection agency or attorney involvement if necessary. Once again, this is not meant as a scare tactic but as a recognition of how seriously you take your relationship with the clients and the obligations you're undertaking.

Additional Information

This section of your contract acts as a request for cooperation from the clients in submitting any information or materials that would be necessary or important in the planning and execution of the event. It doesn't spell out in detail all such requests, but notifies clients that requests may be made for information—and without their timely response, you cannot guarantee the event schedule.

Interpretation

This paragraph acknowledges the creative license and interpretation integral to the event process. It states that as the planner, you'll be using your creative skills to develop the event; once the theme or layout is approved by the clients, you'll proceed accordingly.

Cooperation

Further outlining the dynamics of the event process, this section notes the need for the clients' cooperation with both you and any contracted vendors. It also commits you to the same cooperation.

Change Orders

It's important to formally note that event planning is a dynamic process that may need fre-

The Vendor Contract

Among the duties to specify at the outset for each contract is whether you will serve as the clients' agent and contract on their behalf or whether you will enter into vendor contracts directly. In either case you'll then secure agreements with each vendor. Here are some of the elements that you'll want to include:

- List of all parties involved
- Date
- Load-in time
- Event start time
- Event close time
- Load-out time
- Vendor services
- Event manager services
- Breach of contract
- Independent contractor definition
- Payment to vendor
- Acceptance and signature

quent updates. Known as "change orders," such updates can be issued for signature during the course of planning without invalidating the original contract. Change orders may include additional items or expenses or revisions to the scope of the event. They will also outline any costs associated with these changes.

Important Dates

The date section will formalize the start and end dates of the project. It also validates the time you'll be putting into the planning. This section will complement your production schedule and timelines and show your commitment to the planning process. You might want to insert language such as *expeditious and skillful proceedings* and *use of sufficient labor, materials, equipment, and supplies to bring the event to fruition*. You can also mention reports and schedules to further document event progress.

Delays and Extensions

Reference to delays due to clients, vendors, or causes beyond your own control can be noted here. The communication of delays or of extensions and any necessary alterations in the schedule should be provided verbally and in writing, and guaranteed here. In most situations, an event date is set and you work from the present forward to allocate planning time. It's not typical that an event would be rescheduled due to delays, but additional labor or time may be required if this is the case. This could result in additional costs, which you'd submit to the clients through a change order.

In the event of delays due to clients, you'd request an appropriate extension. This section of your contract could also include reference to any damages you incur because of delays—vendor penalties or forfeited deposits, for instance. You might also wish to note the time frame for settling any expense disputes, and when and if arbitration can be used.

Inspections and Approvals

It's a good idea to show your willingness to have the client participate in any progress inspections during the course of planning. This shows not only your faith in your work, but also your commitment to giving clients what they want. If they should decide to make alterations, it's best to do so as early as possible—*before* you reach the point where it would be costly or inappropriate to make changes. These inspections and approvals may be made during scheduled meetings, or more informally via spot checks of tabletop design, color or material samples, or schematic drawings. They should be documented.

Termination

This section is important for the protection of your client should they ask you to cease performing your duties. Terms for payment to you for services rendered or a refund to your client of any funds paid for work not completed should be spelled out. The client is then free to contract with another planner to complete the project, bearing in mind that you are entitled to compensation for your work, your creativity, and the opportunities you've forgone to devote yourself to this project.

Abandonment

Should the project be abandoned or canceled by the client, this part of the contract protects you up to the amount of time and expenses you've invested to date. It's an unfortunate truth that events will be canceled more often than you'd like. Make sure your contract guarantees you at least partial payment—and try to end on a good note, in the hope that future opportunities for planning arise.

Payment of Fees and Permits

As a planner you'll often find yourself taking out permits or paying fees on behalf of your client. This section acknowledges that such costs may arise. In some instances you're required by law to file for permits—for instance, for tented events, events with pyrotechnics, and events on public property where liquor is being served. It's your responsibility to know what's required for each unique situation, but it's the client's duty to pay or reimburse you for these expenses. (And of course it's always best to avoid advancing expenses in the first place.)

Deviation from Laws and Regulations

You must notify the client in writing about any phases of the event that will deviate from laws or regulations before proceeding with the planning process.

Completion of Event

Here you commit to removing all appropriate items at the close of the event, including equipment, rubbish, or props that were used in the production process.

Indemnity Agreement

You should request that if you incur injury, damage, or claim caused by the conduct of your clients or the attendees at their event, your clients will hold you harmless for any loss you sustain as a result.

Your clients, based on their or their counsel's interpretation and impression, may strike or modify this as well as any of the sections of your contract. If so, I recommend that you in turn consult with your legal counsel and make any necessary modifications to protect your business in the course of your relationship with the client. Depending on the reasonableness of the requested changes, you will probably work to modify the contract and move forward with the project. Many times this provision is made mutual so that each party indemnifies the other. The indemnity provisions must be consistent with your liability insurance policy, particularly when you are asked to name your client or the venue as an additional insured.

Applicable Law

This short statement will define which state's laws will govern the contract—typically the state where your business is located or where the event takes place.

Agreement to Perform

The closing statement commits all parties to perform the covenants stated in the contract. The signature lines, titles of all parties involved, and date follow this brief statement.

A contract like this will prove to be a vital tool for your business. The days when a "gentlemen's handshake" was enough to formalize a relationship are, for better or worse, over. A formal written contract is today the best way to protect both yourself and your clients. It also gives you and your business a professional, reliable aura that will impress your clients event after event!

Permits and Licenses

The terms *permit* and *license* are interchangeable and refer to any permissions that must be issued by governmental authorities for any aspect of an event. When you contract to provide planning services, you will be expected to know what approvals are necessary to perform the event in a safe and legal manner, and you must make it clear whether you or your client will obtain the necessary approval. Never take it for granted that a government authority will issue the approval; you may discover that your request has been denied only days before the event is scheduled to take place.

Such approvals are often required by local, state, or federal agencies in association with gaming activities, parades, demonstrations, tents, street closings, the use of Dumpsters, utilities, the service of food, parking and transportation issues, music use, pyrotechnics, or outdoor signage and banners. Again, it's your responsibility to know which situations warrant prior approval; to know how to secure it; and to make allowances for the time it will take to obtain it.

For example, if you're holding a tented event at which food and alcohol will be served and a fireworks display will close the celebration, you'll need an array of approvals. Begin with the clerk in the city or town hall where the event is being held for information on what boards or agencies will issue each approval. You may have to continue through to federal agencies depending on the situation. If you aren't sure, ask. Discuss each situation with your vendors, venue staff, and fellow professionals. If they provide a service such as food or liquor, they may already have the approvals in place or know where and how to apply.

In situations where music is being used or signage reflecting a copyrighted image is copied, as a planner you must know when such use is appropriate, legal, and ethical and when it isn't. Any copyrighted material may require a license prior to usage. Check with the American Society of Composers, Authors and Publishers (ASCAP), BMI, or a performing rights organization such as SESAC for information on when a license is required and how to get one. Fines and even lawsuits could result if you are ignorant in this area. To run your business as a true professional, take the time to research the proper use of copy-

War Stories: No Signature, No Enlargement

When preparing graphic decor for an anniversary celebration, I proposed using enlarged and mounted photos to decorate the walls of the dining room. My investigative work led me to the prints I wanted, but when I went to enlarge them, I was told by the reproduction company that I needed permission from the original artist or photographer or I would be in copyright infringement. The letters were sent and calls made, and ultimately I got all the necessary approvals to ensure that my creative vision would come to life, but only after much more legwork than I had planned for. A word to the wise: Cover all bases when using anything that's copyrighted, even in the proposal stages!

What It Costs

Attorney Fees: $75–$500 per hour or flat fee for services provided and location

Tax Accountant Fees: typical minimum of $1,200 for general tax preparation services and yearlong consulting advice

General Liability Insurance: $750+ (based on the specialty services you provide, your event experience and track record, and the area you are located in)

Errors and Omissions Insurance: $3,000+

Lawsuit by Client or Guest: Varies widely

righted material. Your client will respect you for your knowledge and prudence.

Insurance

Despite all your contractual and risk management precautions, your liability exposure cannot be completely eliminated. Thus, make it a point to review with your insurance specialist what business coverage you should have. Let's take a look at the array of business insurance policies available. First acknowledge that you are the key to the success of your business. Life insurance, health insurance, disability insurance, and key person insurance would all apply to you as business owner. You should consider comprehensive general liability and property insurance at the very least, with options for other specialty policies such as cancellation insurance, employment practices insurance, and/or business interruption

insurance. If you have employees, most states require workers' compensation insurance, which you cannot avoid by calling someone you hire, yet control, a subcontractor. You may also choose to purchase errors and omissions insurance to cover you for claims against your business for errors you may make in the course of rendering the professional service of event planning. These are but a few of the many insurance options available.

Locate a broker who comes well recommended with experience in plans for small businesses, home-based businesses, or event or meeting management companies. A trusted adviser can walk you through the pros and cons as well as the cost and feasibility of taking out each policy for you and your company.

Attorney James Decoulos suggests becoming aware of the standards slowly developing in the event industry. Failure to comply with these standards can lead to liability problems. The Accepted Practices Exchange (APEX) project of the Convention Industry Council has been reviewing and developing industry standards that could be the yardstick against which such claims are measured. Familiarize yourself with APEX and consider these issues in your risk management and insurance programs. You can find more about the APEX initiative and progress from your local industry, event, and meeting groups or online using the key words "Accepted Practices Exchange."

Ask your insurance adviser about the special risks you face as both a home-based business owner and an event planner. Bring your coverage up to date to avoid legal or financial disaster.

War Stories: Oops!

A gala event nearly created more drama than expected when an oversized vase holding a massive floral arrangement burst during setup. The designer was whisked off to the hospital to receive stitches, returning in time to make finishing touches before the event began. Be very careful of containers, especially those that are in poor condition or fragile.

At another tented event the designer set tall frond-laden vases filled with fresh fruits on top of mirror bases. When the winds picked up, the vases began to topple, pouring water and fruits out onto the lovely tablecloths. Luckily, I stumbled onto the scene in time to grab some "gaffer" tape (specialty lighting tape) and tape all of the vases in place; I then concealed this precautionary measure with some scattered floral buds. It is always wise to consider all conditions, even if it means stepping down the "look" of the design just a bit!

Improving Your Risk Exposure

This overview of the legal and risk implications that you face as a planner may reveal areas in your own procedures that need review and attention. If you don't have a contract you feel is thorough enough, revisit it. Find a legal adviser who's savvy about special events and seek advice on preparing your documents so you and your client are approaching your relationship professionally.

Become more critical of the way you produce your events. Are the electrical wires or extension cords taped down so guests don't trip? Are any open flames located well away from loose fabric or decorations? Does the fabric you use meet local or state fire codes? Are all your permits and your vendors' permits in place? Are you using insured vendors? Are you named as an additional insured on their policy for the specific event date you contract with them? Do you risk fire or explosion from the materials you use or the way you present them? Is security in place for the safety of guests? Do you meet any state or federal regulations concerning the Americans with Disabilities Act or other mandated laws for public events?

Creating a Risk Assessment Plan

Work through a risk assessment plan for each event. How likely is it that an accident or injury might occur? Think about:

- Location
- Guest profile
- Decor
- Entertainment
- Transportation
- Cuisine and beverage service
- Lighting and production services
- Safety and security
- Evacuation procedures

Will your entertainment require any staging or rigging? How will you move people from one location to another? Consider your food preparation and storage. Examine how clearly fire exits are marked, and what evacuation procedures are in place.

These are just a small sampling of the questions you should ask yourself as you plan each event. Depending on the size, location, and type

War Stories: Precooked and Ready to Blow!

A catering manager shares this story about a colleague who was running late for a job: "His truck was loaded, but he knew with traffic he'd be cutting it really close. In the interest of time, he decided to light the Sterno units under the chafing dishes in the back of the truck to start the heating process. As the caterer was driving, he noticed black smoke coming from inside the cab. Yes, he did catch the truck on fire. Luckily he was able to put the fire out and still made it to the job." It's better to make it to the job late than not make it at all! It's never worth taking chances.

of event you're planning, not all issues will be weighed equally. Still, I hope I have given you a sense of the seriousness of your task as a planner and the risk you assume when you accept the responsibility of overseeing an event. If some of this seems overwhelming, I suggest taking a course or completing an education session at an industry conference that deals specifically with risk and legal issues. Regulations and requirements are changing by the minute and vary from state to state, city to city. The most responsible and professional position to take is to be prepared. Know what your legal and contractual obligations are for the safe and smooth production of your events.

Event Ethics

Ethical behavior in our society is continually under scrutiny. Whether you're a high-level official with the ability to touch the lives of thousands or an event planner who works with a few clients and vendors, you are responsible for your actions and how they affect others.

In 1987 a group of event professionals joined together and formed the International Special Events Society under the direction of Dr. Joe Jeff Goldblatt, CSEP. Upon becoming a member of ISES, participants in the group agreed to adhere to the ISES Principles of Professional Conduct and Ethics. Among other things this means that each member will "promote and encourage the highest level of ethics within the profession of the special events industry."

The fact that our industry is insisting its members consistently do the right thing can only enhance our reputation among the public. Still, ethics often involve moral considerations that can differ across cultures, geographic locations, circumstances, and professions. In other words, the questions and decisions you face in your business may not always be easy ones.

Ethical Quandaries

- Gift giving and accepting
- Taking credit for other people's creative ideas
- Failure to acknowledge others' contributions to your events
- Use of others' material in your promotional work
- Payment policies: commissions or kickbacks?

When you consider your own standards, take a look at the mission statement you created in your business plan. What elements can you reflect on during the event planning process? As you negotiate with vendors or clients, are you behaving in a manner that you are proud of? Are the gifts or compensation you receive necessary to your work? Do they affect your ability to make sound, unprejudiced decisions?

We are in a highly creative field, and it's sometimes difficult to protect our unique ideas. We share them with clients and colleagues in the proposal process and during networking events. Few experiences are more disheartening than presenting a fabulous theme and ideas for execution to clients—who then fail to hire you and put on the event themselves. As frustrating as this may seem, you must realize that ideas alone are not legally protected and do not themselves make the event successful. Instead, it's all the components that transform an event from a piece of paper into reality that count. It's the risk assessment, the attention to detail, the wealth of information on sources for products and services, and the way you as a professional planner are able to carry it all out to perfection. It's the training and attention to building your business that allow you be an event creator, not merely someone who follows an instruction booklet.

There are no right or wrong answers to some ethical questions. It is up to you to make the choices you're proud of and that represent professional behavior as you understand it.

Frequently Asked Questions

I have just presented a terrific event plan to a client. How can I prevent them from going ahead and implementing it without hiring me as the planner?

First, don't let too much of your idea out of the bag. Give them broad strokes of your thematic elements, and then emphasize the implementation process you will oversee. Second, consider charging for doing a proposal, especially if it involves a creative component. If you sense that the prospect wants a very detailed description, then enter into a contract at the outset that provides for a fee for the proposal, which will be credited if you are hired as the planner.

I am halfway through planning a wedding, and the bride and groom have split. How much should I expect to get paid, and can I get reimbursed for the down payments I have made to vendors?

This is a matter of contract. You should expect to get paid for everything that you have done and get reimbursed for all your obligations to your vendors. Progress payments should be consistent with your performance, and you should be attentive that they are made in a timely fashion.

I have a client who has started going directly to my vendors for events and cutting me out of the picture! How can I avoid this?

Your contract should note that your client should not contract directly with your vendors, and likewise your vendor contract should state that they will not contract directly with your client. However, your contracts cannot obligate your client and your vendors indefinitely for future events. It is best to work with vendors who know where their bread is buttered and that you will not give them work in the future if they contract directly with your client. Ethically, it would make sense that they respect the parameters of a client/vendor relationship and support you in this. Similarly, be on the lookout for clients who are contracting behind your back. This could also create limited revenue for you if you charge on a percentage basis as they contract for higher-priced services directly and cut you out of the action.

Am I required to pay for health insurance or workers' compensation for my contract labor?

That depends upon whether your contract laborers are truly independent. If you control not only what they do, but also how they do it, the worker is an employee and you are responsible for all benefits as well as payroll tax withholdings. Workers' compensation auditors often assess an audit premium for contract laborers who do not have their own workers' compensation and liability insurance. Sometimes, this can be challenged;

Frequently Asked Questions (continued)

however, if those contract laborers have employees who are not covered by their workers' compensation, you will be required to do so, even if they are only contracted by you. It is best to hire contract labor with their own insurance and keep a current copy of their certificates of insurance on file. Your contract should require them to do so.

Should I go to contract with every client, even if it is a last-minute job or a small piece of business? What about changes in their requirements?

There should be a written contract for every job, no matter how little the lead time is or how small the job is. There's no reason in these days of e-mail capability for failing to forward your contract as an attachment and request that it be completed and e-mailed back to you—and then preferably that it be signed and faxed or mailed back. At least send an e-mail with the details of performance and payment in the body of the e-mail and request a confirmation reply that includes the legal name and address of your client and the full name of the individual stating the nature of the authority to contract for your client.

You've got your crisp business card and letterhead; your office is complete with desk, phone, and fax. You've made it clear to family and friends that you're serious about your passion. You've honed your skills through job experience, volunteerism, and education. You're ready to begin planning your first event.

If you're coming from a job or position in which you're used to seeing only one part of the event process, it will be important for you to get the full snapshot of what a client will expect when you sign on to plan your first event. Even if you choose to focus on only one area of events, knowledge of the steps from concept to completion is a good idea.

Whether you get your business from referrals or call-ins from a yellow pages ad, most clients will expect a presentation of some sort on what the event will look like. A true professional will do this in writing with graphics, diagrams, or photographs to support the descriptions of the event elements. This first step, the proposal, can be broad or very detailed; it can also give options from which clients may select their final choices. Whether it's a simple birthday party or a lavish fundraiser, the proposal will begin the formal process of your relationship with the client and should be treated thoughtfully.

Facts and Figures
"Proposal Elements" lists the basic information you should try to include in every proposal; if you feel you must add other information, do so. Some clients have great imaginations and can picture, from your verbal and written descriptions, how an event will look. I have found

Proposal Elements

Purpose of event

Guest list profile

Event specifics

Event description and theme presentation

Decor elements

Entertainment

Cuisine

Tangibles

Cost analysis presentation

Evaluation measures/goal recap

this to be the exception, however, rather than the rule. Most clients know they want a fabulous affair, but have no idea how to get there. That's why need the help of a pro! Take the time to describe and support all the elements of your proposal, and your clients will feel more comfortable with their decision to hire you.

Purpose of Event

Step one is to state the purpose of the event. Why are your clients spending the money and taking the time to create this event? This very basic step will spell out the event's goals and give you a tool to measure its success. Is it a birthday celebration, a gathering to build company spirit, an evening of recognition, or an opportunity to showcase a facility? Take time to explore the clients' expectations and you will better match each element in

the design phase. You may want to add a brief description of the style of the host or hostess, or the corporate culture as you see it. This will allow the client to comment on your accuracy and provide additional, valuable information to help with your creative development.

Guest List Profile

Who will be attending? List the number of guests, their ages, and their profiles. Will spouses and children attend? Will this be an affair open to the general public? Will you set a limit on attendees? Will you need special services based on age profiles? Will you need to please a broad spectrum of ages and tastes with the food and entertainment you select?

Clarifying these elements reveals your knowledge of the planning process. It also makes clear that the needs of the clients will drive all of an event's ingredients. Think about risk analysis, security and wheelchair-accessibility procedures, a variety of entertainment options . . . everything you need (based on the guest profile) to create a safe and successful event. When you reach the budget and cost phase, you can show how your pricing closely reflects meeting guests' needs and supports why you may be including some elements.

Event Specifics

List the items that are set in concrete. *The client only has $10,000 to spend. It must be held from 11:00 A.M. to 4:00 P.M. on a Saturday in June.* With these and any other givens in place, you can then explore the options available under these circumstances. You'll quickly eliminate venues that are previously booked, cuisine selections that are out of budget, or themes that don't make sense for the particular event. Remember, pay close attention to your clients' desires throughout the proposal phase.

Event Description and Theme Presentation

Here's where you pull out all stops and strut your stuff. You've clarified your clients' wishes, and you'll present to them your plan for how you'll carry out all their dreams and desires. You should select one theme as your primary one—but be prepared to shift if this isn't received well. Your event elements will support your theme through decor, entertainment, and catering.

Decor Elements

How will you bring your theme to life? Dig deep into the "whys" of the event to present a theme that is innovative and will reach the clients' goals. This is one place to insert photo images of your suggestions. It will help your clients visualize your thematic plan. Don't forget a full description of linens, florals, entry decor, bathroom appointments, and so on, to secure the image in your clients' minds.

Entertainment

This very important element—the life of the party—will naturally flow from the event's givens and guest profile. The selections you recommend for music, dancing, or performance-based entertainment should all reflect the purpose for the event. Budget, of course, will drive many of your

selections as well. Don't forget entertainers who may greet guests, circulate among them, or serve as event highlights.

Cuisine

Hot dogs or filet mignon, plated or buffet, full seated dinner or buffet-style hors d'oeurvres . . . your recommendations should fit both the budget and the concept of your clients' event. Creative food presentations and descriptions are a great way to show your flair and capabilities as a professional planner. Consult with trusted catering managers for the latest in food and serving trends.

Tangibles

From invitations to parting mementos, tangible items may be featured at the event that must tie into the theme or purpose. Here's where your file cabinet or e-mail "favorites" folder can be perused

War Stories: The Client Is Always Right

I was hired to produce a celebration for a sweet sixteen birthday. Although this couple could easily afford the most lavish of treatments for the party, they were concerned that they might appear ostentatious and frivolous at a time when family budgets were being tightened. I presented elements that supported their wishes, such as invitations that were traditionally shaped yet still produced in a modern and creative way, thus meeting the clients' needs but still delivering a unique and fun result.

Project Estimation Sheet

Task	Est. Hours	Actual Hours	Rate
Administrative			
Proposal/contracting			
Memos/corrrespondence			
Budgeting			
Evaluation			
Billing			
Event Management			
Venue selection/visits			
Vendor evaluation/pricing			
Vendor management			
Project management			
Timelines/production schedules			
Promotion			
Print/invitations			
Promotional items			
Risk Assessment and Monitoring			
Legal documents/contracts			
Guest needs			
Vendor quality control			
Venue inspection			
Safety plans			
Safety enhancements			

for just the right novelty or print piece. Relying on good vendors can also be a time-saving way to stay up on the latest and greatest in these specialty areas. Kevin Powers from SwervePoint, who handles specialty incentives, and Bonny Katzman of BK Designs, a premier invitation designer, are always there to give me the latest in trends in their areas of focus. Keep some reliable sources on hand, and it will put you at the top when it comes time for supporting your event with these items.

Cost Analysis

After you've laid out the who, when, why, where, and what . . . it's time for the "how much." This should not come as a shocking surprise to your client. Many times, people will be evasive when discussing budget: "I don't know, just tell me how much it will cost." If you've firmed up all of an event's other components with them—style, purpose, guest list—but the issue of money is left dangling, use your professional skill to set a price and go for it. On rare occasions I've seen clients completely floored to learn that in order to host an outdoor event, the cost of tenting, lighting, portable lavatories, tables, and chairs had to be figured in. Most of the time, however, the clients who ask for filet mignon know what it'll cost and are prepared to pay for it.

Sometimes event decision making is handled by a committee—and this can be very time consuming. In this case I suggest charging an hourly fee for the proposal and event feasibility phase. Spell this out in a contract, and you'll be compensated for the education process that you offer the board on the cost and planning procedures of a special event. If the event doesn't come to fruition, you'll be covered for your time and expenses.

The budget should include all elements of the event. The best tactic is to include all elements in broad categories, then break things down additionally on a per-person basis. In the proposal phase you can be general, but remember to figure in all your costs for labor, permitting, security, transportation, rentals, and so on, so that you don't have to come back later with revisions. You may not get an increased budget after the fact. It's also better to bring in a lower cost at contract-signing time, rather than a higher one.

Evaluation Measures/Goal Recap

In the final paragraph, state how you plan to measure your success at reaching event goals. Some of these evaluation procedures can be subjective: *People had a good time, guests stayed to the closing remarks, people crowded the dance floor.* Others can be noted objectively: *Employee turnover decreased, people accepted overtime assignments, donations for the auction items were up 40 percent from the prior year.* Measures for evaluation might include questionnaires or surveys filled out on paper at the event, or via postcard or e-mail afterward. The shorter and more concise and specific, the better. It could be helpful to offer an incentive for responses—perhaps the respondents' names can be entered into a drawing for a grand prize. You may mention suggestions for evaluation in your proposal. This is a great way to generate ongoing business and show your commitment to helping your clients get results. If it worked out this year, they may want to do it again in the future.

Timelines

Another important part of your planning process is creating a timeline for your team and your clients. This crucial planning tool helps you keep your project on target and keep expectations clear throughout the process. Start with a month-by-month plan of activities, then shorten the time increments as the event date draws near. Outline the tasks involved and the parties responsible for them. This allows you to monitor progress and identify expectations. It will also help you budget your time and show your clients your progress month by month. This timeline will partner nicely with your production schedule, which serves as your event implementation and management tool. (I'll turn to the production schedule shortly!)

In the best-case scenario, you will have ample time to prepare and plan for each client's event. Sometimes, however—and more often than we'd like—we are called on to create an event in a short period of time. Here are two scenarios, one with a four-month lead time and another with a twelve-month planning schedule.

Sample Fund-Raiser Timeline and Services Overview: Four-Month Lead Time

Four months prior to the event:
- Discuss budget.
- Explore support (guest list compilation, key sponsor list).
- Formulate theme and complementary print pieces.
- Create detailed timeline and production schedule draft.
- Research vendors, raw materials, cost and production of invitations.
- Review database/compile guest list.

Three months prior:
- Finalize guest list.
- Develop theme for use throughout the event.
- Review venue and service providers (entertainment, props, food services, transportation, lighting, AV).
- Create invitation and complementary print structure (brochure, incentives, signage).
- Sponsor management.

- Publicity: Create press release and explore press coverage pre- and post-event.
- Raffle items: Decide on donations, purchased items, sponsored items.

Two months prior:
- Review and order placement of giveaway items.
- Continue review and updating of vendor services (contracts, deposits, orders, logistics).
- Hold management and planning meetings.
- Manage publicity including follow-up.

Six weeks prior:
- Print and mail invitations.
- Database management: monitor RSVPs, special needs, transportation, update info.
- Continue review and updating of vendor services (contracts, deposits, orders, logistics).
- Hold management and planning meetings.

Four weeks prior:
- Continue managing guest list.
- Continue vendor management (deposits, logistics, scheduling).
- Continue signage and print support.
- Work on staffing and scheduling.
- Hold management and planning meetings.

Two weeks prior:
- Finalize guest list (gifts, VIP lists, transportation, hospitality).
- Finalize timeline and production schedule.
- Review and confirm all event activities: vendors (entertainment, rentals, photography/videography, props, decor), publicity, parking, staffing, food services, sponsorship, raffles, gifts.
- Hold final meetings and walk-through.

Event date:
- Conduct on-site management of event and post-event review.

Sample Corporate Timeline: Twelve-Month Lead Time

12–16 months out:

- Formulation of theme and complementary print pieces
- Venue walk-through and initial layout discussion
- Review of service providers:

    Vendors

    > Entertainment
    >
    > Rentals
    >
    > Photography
    >
    > Videography
    >
    > Props/decor
    >
    > Linens
    >
    > Lighting
    >
    > AV

    Publicity

    Gifts

    Parking/transportation

    Security

    Staffing

    Food services

    Sponsorships: purveyor partnerships

    Raffles

- Creation of detailed timeline and production schedule draft
- Research into vendors, raw materials, cost and production of invitations
- Database review/guest list
- Finalization of guest list
- Demo room: Investigation of equipment

10–12 weeks out:

- Management and planning meetings
- Creation of invitation and complementary print structure/final proof
- Giveaways: Review and final selection of giveaway items
- Demo room: Plan setup and supplies/staffing

8 weeks out:
- Management and planning meetings
- Publicity: Press coverage pre- and post-event
- Giveaways: Order placement
- Printing and mailing of invitations (envelopes)
- Raffle items: Donations, purchased items, sponsored items
- Partner management

7 weeks out:
- Vendor confirmation
    - Contract
    - Deposit
    - Orders

6 weeks out:
- Management and planning meetings
- Decor
- Table props
- Signage: Entryway, demo room, event flow, raffles, history

5 weeks out:
- Management and planning meetings
- Food service planning
- Continued review and updating of vendor services (contracts, deposits, orders, logistics)
- Database management: Monitoring RSVP, special needs, transportation, updating info

4 weeks out:
- Management and planning meetings
- Signage development/schedule of events
- Database management

3 weeks out:

- Management and planning meetings
- Staffing and scheduling
- Giveaways: Receipt and packaging
- Final production schedule
- Final event schedule

2 weeks out:

- Final timeline and production schedule
- Review and confirm all event activities:

    Vendors

    Entertainment

    Rentals

    Photography

    Videography

    Props/decor

    Publicity

    Parking/transportation

    Staffing

    Food services

    Sponsorships

    Raffles

    Gifts

- Final guest list (gifts, VIP lists, transportation, hospitality, name badges)
- Name badge printing

1 week out:

- Final meetings and walk-through
- Technical walk-throughs

Event date:

- On-site management

1 week after:

- Post-event review

Sample Social Event Production Schedule

Location _____

Date _____

Time	Staff	Activity
10:00 A.M.		Arrive for initial setup with florals, supplies, linens, bathroom amenities
		Walk-through with hostess for parking, setup, delivery
		Review of teardown time and staging locations
10:00 A.M.–noon	Rental company	Deliver four high-top cocktail tables
noon	Production/lighting company	Arrive and begin installation of production, lighting, video
2:00 P.M.	Balloon vendor	Arrive with inflated balloons and begin installation
3:00 P.M.	Caterer	Arrive and begin setup and installation of food/equipment
4:00 P.M.	Planner/project manager	Buffets dressed
5:00 P.M.	Planner/project manager	Tables dressed/decor in place
	Balloon vendor	Setup complete/depart
6:00 P.M.	All vendors	Pre-event walk-through
	Planner/project manager	Staff for check-in prepped
7:00 P.M.		Guests begin to arrive
	Vendors	In place for start of event
	Planner/project manager	Gate, coat, and shoe check-in staff in place
9:00 P.M.	Planner/project manager	Check-in staff departs
midnight	Vendors	Event ends/teardown begins

Time	Activity
7:00 A.M.	Breakfast
8:00 A.M.	Signage setup
	Room check: beverage, AV, tables/chairs
9:00 A.M.	Photographer, videographer meeting (content, key people, objectives)
10:00 A.M.	Security in place
	Speaker dry runs: See speaker schedule
11:00 A.M.	Voice mail to each sponsor/exhibitor re meeting at 5:00, post-show meeting, overview and etiquette, objectives (get room)
	Voice mail to each staff person re preshow meeting
noon	Solution room move-in
1:00 P.M.	Review special event lineup: entertainment needs (prep room, food services, special needs), decor
2:00 P.M.	Coordinate room drops
3:00 P.M.	Emcee and executive meeting: briefing
4:00 P.M.	Sponsor/exhibitor meeting
5:00 P.M.	Special event setup: decor, band, banquet/dining tables, food services
6:00 P.M.	Preshow meeting: show etiquette and conference overview and schedule
7:00 P.M.	Special event begins
8:00 P.M.	CEO gives toast, recognizes and introduces sponsor
9:00 P.M.	Sponsor speaks
10:00 P.M.	Event ends

Making It Happen

The production schedule serves to record all activities necessary to fully prepare for the event. It will help you think through all the steps in the event planning process. It should list each activity, what time it needs to take place, and who is responsible. Activities such as deliveries, setup, staging, and teardown should be noted. All parties involved should have this schedule and know when they fit in and what their responsibilities are. You can note any task you must do—think of it as the "Master To-Do" list.

For example, in order for guests to enjoy their meal, you will have tables delivered and set up; linens ordered, delivered, and laid (and packaged for pickup after the event as well); serviceware ordered, delivered, and set (then cleaned and returned after the event); centerpieces made, delivered, and positioned; food and beverages ordered and prepared; and your staff oriented and in place to serve. And these are just a few elements of your entire event; other issues may include getting licenses or permits, organizing speaker transportation and briefings, taking care of electrical wiring and fire safety, and brushing up on parking regulation. You should prepare a moment-by-moment detailed list and assign someone to make sure every item is carried out. In the beginning you may be doing it all yourself, or assigning a production manager this responsibility. Don't leave anything out of your production schedule!

Production schedules will differ from event to event. A tented wedding will require a longer list of vendors than a small social event hosted in your clients' home. Still, every schedule must include all preparations, a complete vendor list, delivery schedules, setup and teardown plans, and how messages will be communicated to all parties. The previous samples can be broken down even further, if you wish, depending on the number of activities, the number of vendors, and the size of the event.

The Critical Elements of Every Event
Theme and Concept Development

The theme of the event is one of the first and most important elements in the development process. Many times your effectiveness in presenting and executing your theme will be the deciding factor in getting you a planning project. The way you develop your theme shows your creativity, experience, and intellect.

You should approach theme development in an adventuresome way, but remember that not all clients may be as daring as you. Sometimes it can take a while for clients to learn to trust your suggestions, and they may need added assurance to fully embrace your creative concepts. You may need to balance your creative urges against your clients' tolerance levels, too: If you have very conservative clients, you may not want to suggest a burlesque show as the main entertainment. On the other hand if your clients have planned several failed fund-raisers with cheese and crackers as the main course, it may be time for them to think sushi and cosmos! Thoughtful fact finding with your client during the initial stages will guide you on the right direction.

Customer Service

Depending on the type of event planning you provide, you may have clients for a short time, as you would in planning a wedding, or you may be developing long-term relationships with corporate and other clients. Building these relationships may require meetings or lunches that give you a chance to get to know your clients—their tastes, their hot buttons, and how you can create events they'll be proud of. Creating a reputation in this manner takes time, but it's what determines how satisfied your clients are at the end of the day.

I typically schedule check-in meetings with my clients during the event planning process to share ideas or samples. I also set up visits to discuss change orders or last-minute requests. I check in with the client during the event itself and, most importantly, plan for a follow-up or evaluation meeting. This gives me a nice overview of the whole process and helps me make sure that all my clients get what they want.

Moreover, this frequent contact is what will give you your follow-up business, because it creates happy clients willing to use you again or refer you to others. Time spent on the client relationship may be the most important investment you can make in your business.

Location

Budget, convenience, size of the group, time of year, theme choice, and many other factors can drive the selection of the event location. Often clients will look to you for suggestions and advice on selecting an appropriate venue. Turn to your lists of venues you've inspected as well as recommendations from colleagues and vendors to suggest the right fit for each project.

Some locations will require additional on-site services—for example, a tented event on the water's edge. Permitting, rain date planning, toilet facilities, and lighting are just a few of the additional services needed to make a tent environment safe and enjoyable. Other venues will offer one-stop shopping, even nearby sleeping rooms, as in a hotel ballroom. Once again, the initial fact-seeking meeting should give you some clues as to what direction your clients would like to go.

Guest List

Typically, your clients will compile the guest list. In some cases, such as in a fund-raising event, clients may request assistance in achieving attendance goals. This enters into a very different level of responsibilities and should be treated as a separate function from the event planning and management services you will provide. I'll cover the unique features of nonprofit events in chapter 11.

The guest list will affect the cost of the event and could drive other decisions you make in the production process. As a full-service planner, you may offer to provide database management and/or mailing services. Should you decide to do this, just remember that saying, *Time is money.* Estimate or keep track of the time you spend providing these extras and charge your clients accordingly. If clients prefer not to be involved with this phase of the planning process, your attention to this detail will ensure a correct headcount and help with the final planning stages.

Resources Needed

Vendors

The cuisine you recommend for an event should come after thoughtful consideration of budget, theme, and guest profile. Having a solid list of caterers who can fit your various needs and budget is essential. Keep your preferred caterers' availability, pricing, and menu suggestions in mind during the proposal and contracting phase. Even though this may mean more research and time for you before the project is finalized, it will mean fewer surprises and misunderstandings in this very important part of the event.

The same is true for other event vendors such as entertainment, decor, rentals, and production services. Dig into your tool chest and peruse your collection of flyers, brochures, advertisements, and other marketing materials from vendors or competitors. If you're used to doing quick Internet searches to find products and services, don't discount the effectiveness of photographs, articles, or magazine clippings, which can offer a more visual experience when you're digging for ideas or inspiration. A thorough knowledge of vendors' pricing structure, availability, and capabilities will let you deliver what you promise. A quick call or e-mail to double-check such information will save you time and possibly your reputation in the long run.

Staffing

As you walk through the event, from planning through setup to teardown, don't forget the labor and staffing needs you may have. You may con-

> **War Stories: Covering All the Bases**
>
> Even after you've held a pre-event meeting and assigned all the event tasks to the proper staff, it pays to double-check and make sure that everyone is clear about their duties and the equipment they're responsible for. At a large tented event in Newport, Rhode Island, one catering manager learned this lesson the hard way. The truck from the catering facility was all packed up, everything ready to go. The operations manager asked the driver, who was fairly new, to bring the truck around, and they'd be on their way. After driving the hour or so to the site, they opened the roll door to the truck . . . to find it completely empty. Apparently, the new driver had brought the wrong truck around—the empty one rather than the full one. Whoops!

sider outsourcing to professional specialty staffing companies for wait staff, security personnel, or valet service. Or you might prefer to bring in your trusted contract pros to handle the specific jobs needed. Remember to figure these items into your price proposal. Don't forget any management and training time you may need to set aside.

As you coordinate the support staff and vendors, your role as a manager becomes even more critical. Putting your stamp on the event, and "inspecting what you expect," includes sharing your vision, training, delivering clear and concise expectations, and developing evaluation measures to let your hired help know how they performed. Taking the time to think through the process and how you will qualify success is critical in building your reputation and your company. It will also help your vendors to work effectively with you for future events and build strong relationships with both vendors and clients.

Marketing Your Events

Whether by invitation only or through paid admission, every event has a marketing component. The first step of announcing the event may take shape through a save-the-date card one year before a wedding, or through advertising a fundraising event in a local newspaper. Assisting your client in planning their marketing campaign will include pricing, thematic development and flow, multimedia options, gifts and give-aways, and branding. Consideration should also be given to protocol and hospitality to fit your client's style and event goals. From the initial presentation of your event to the follow-up thank-you notes, the marketing of your event will help your client maximize attendance and achieve the event goals.

Taking Precautions

Whenever you open your arms and doors to guests, it is always wise to think of any special needs or provisions you might take to make their experience most pleasurable. For social events, your clients may know when special arrange-ments are needed for guests with disabilities or dietary restrictions. These are usually easier to identify and determined by the host or hostess. In public events, as an event planner, it is imperative to consider the legal implications of offering fair access to all participants (the Americans with Disabilities Act requires compliance in public events) and taking precautions for safe execution of all aspects of the event. Festivals and citywide events open planners up to a wide array of compliance and safety issues. It is wise to prepare fully when undertaking events of this nature to protect both the client and yourself. Legal implications of events can include proper contracting, licensing, permitting, and compliance with all local, state, and federal regulations. It also includes taking business insurance and ethics seriously and covering all bases before the event begins.

Event Evaluation

It bears repeating that the evaluation of your event is crucial both for you as a planner and for your clients. It will help you improve your services and also help substantiate your value as a planner. In all phases of the event planning process, evaluating the success of your proposal, your training and staffing, your marketing, your execution, and your attention to the details of safety and risk management will make the difference in success for your event and for you as a planner.

Frequently Asked Questions

How much should I spend to create a proposal?

It depends on the client and the scope of the project. A PowerPoint presentation made from your laptop with photos and diagrams may be appropriate for the corporate client. Multiple bound, tabbed binders presented to the board of directors for a nonprofit might make an impressive statement. Find out who will attend the meeting and how many other companies are bidding, and ask them what they prefer before you spend the time, energy, and money on creating something that they would not appreciate.

Are production schedules really necessary?

From setup schedules for equipment and rentals, to time for the caterer to arrive, prep food, and heat up the ovens . . . all the preparations should be clearly laid out so everyone is ready to go when the party begins. Ordering monogrammed materials or securing permitting from local authorities for tenting needs may take more time than you realize, so make sure your schedule starts well in advance so no one is disappointed. If you develop a production schedule from the beginning, you can add in all the details to make sure nothing is left out.

Does every event need marketing materials?

You would not necessarily think of a wedding as needing "marketing materials," but consider how you will help your client present the event to the guests. Information from save-the-date cards to in-room welcome cards listing the schedule of events would be appropriate to develop for a social client. Professionally printed materials may work for corporate or nonprofit clients while a computer-generated and copied flyer would be acceptable for a school fund-raiser or community dance. Base your suggestions for marketing materials on the client, budget, and culture of the event to develop print or advertising materials that are a perfect match.

Do I need to worry about what resources my vendors need?

Absolutely! If you have a lighting company providing decor lighting, you will need to know what power they will need and make sure your venue has this available. If it is a tented event, you may need to secure a generator. Once the band, the caterer, and the lighting company all tie in, you may blow a fuse and end the party in one flip of a switch! Other needs include tables for caterers to prep on or a DJ to set their equipment on. You may need to consider listing a section in your vendor contract that asks them to detail what their needs will be including food, rentals, services, or utilities.

Social Celebrations: Weddings and More

Planning social events can be one of the most exciting areas of event planning. You're helping bring people's dreams to life! Weddings, anniversaries, bar and bat mitzvahs, showers, and other celebratory events mark milestones in people's lives. For those who are completely overwhelmed by the thought of inviting six people to a dinner party, let alone organizing an event for a hundred, an event planner becomes an indispensable partner—not only by imparting a knowledge of the planning process, but by juggling the many traditions, vendors, and details as well as offering advice with the often overwhelming decisions the social client will have to make.

The Joys of Planning Social Events

One benefit to specializing in social events is that people will always have milestones in their lives that they want to celebrate: from births, through religious celebrations like baptisms, to the teenage years of bar mitzvahs and birthdays, followed by engagements, weddings, anniversaries, housewarming parties, bon voyage parties, and retirement parties! Your relationship with any given social client can be long and lucrative if cultivated properly.

Another benefit is the recession-proof nature of the social market. Although spending may be cut back in slow economic times, milestones still occur. After the tragedy of September 11, we saw a trend toward "don't wait to celebrate," and more weddings and celebrations were scheduled. While planning cycles may be shortened in tough economic times, and budgets may be shaved, the social client still wants all the pomp and circumstance to commemorate special moments. To

Why Plan Social Events?

- The business is recession-proof, at least to a degree: The general public will always have milestones to celebrate.
- You can get referrals from satisfied clients and vendors for other social projects.
- You can be as creative as you like.
- Once you know your way around social events, you can become a pro at all types of them: weddings, bar mitzvahs, and so on, and so on.

be successful as a social planner, you should be creative with your use of and suggestions for event elements—and firm with your fee and service structure.

If managed properly, the social client can be a built-in marketing resource. Referrals from satisfied clients can be invaluable for getting future projects. Don't overlook satisfied vendors and facility managers. If you do your job properly and cultivate good relationships, you can set the stage for ongoing business. It makes vendors' jobs easier if they know a reliable planner is handling the details. Follow up with a card of thanks after an event to keep your name on the tips of their tongues for other social projects.

Creative Themes

A full palette of social clients will let you push the limit of your creative prowess. If you're planning

bar and bat mitzvahs in a particular area, you can be sure the guests attending will want to see fresh themes and ideas at each event. The guest lists for these events could overlap from party to party, because many of the children may be friends and will want to share in each other's celebrations. Once you're established as a social planner with a certain clientele, you'll become a valuable resource to the entertaining community.

Similar Processes

While all events share basic elements, some social events have additional unique features that you should be familiar with. Wedding traditions, for instance, include the processional, ceremony con-

Types of Social Celebrations

- Weddings
- Anniversaries
- Bar and bat mitzvahs
- Religious ceremonies
- Baptisms
- Confirmations
- Birthdays
- Engagement parties
- Bachelor and bachelorette parties
- Galas
- Bon voyage parties
- Housewarming parties
- Holiday parties
- Seasonal celebrations

tent, recessional, reception with party introductions, cutting of the cake, and special dances. Once you're comfortable with the flow, you can be a valuable resource to new brides who don't have a clue to what they should be doing and when. Do be prepared to learn the various wedding nuances based on religion, social customs, and ethnic traditions before you commit to planning a specialized ceremony.

Social Planning Pitfalls

Of course, it's not all sunshine as a social planner. One challenging component can be dealing with the strong emotions that arise throughout the planning process. It's a time of hope, fear, frustration, expectation, and elation. Brides and grooms are preparing for one of the most special moments of their lifetime, and mothers and fathers are preparing for a major life change in their relationship with their children. Knowing this, you must handle issues delicately so as not to offend or escalate the natural volatile state of the social client.

In social events, especially in weddings, there is a tendency to have multiple managers—mother of the bride, father of the bride, bride, groom, even stepparents and bridesmaids. Some of these people will have an impact on the financial management, others on the flow of the event or the design ideas. It's important to keep things in perspective and try to pinpoint the one person who is the final decision maker. *A word of caution:* This may not be the person who initially hired you! Be prepared to be flexible and open to change during the planning process.

Wedding Checklist

Rehearsal:
- Ceremony rehearsal
- Rehearsal dinner

Getting ready:
- Hair
- Makeup
- Clothing (bridal party)
- Rentals
- Snacks

Ceremony:
- Justice of the peace
- Musical ensemble
- Bridal party
- Florals
- Rentals
- Decor

Reception:
- Decor
- Florals
- Entertainment
- Photo session
- Cocktail hour
- Party introductions
- First dance
- Family dance
- Dinner/food
- Cutting of the cake
- Garter/bouquet toss
- Socializing and dancing
- Wedding party departure

Budget Constraints

One very important skill a planner must have is the ability to balance dreams with reality. This is especially true when it comes to budgeting. All events are driven by a budget. The higher it is, the more choices you'll be able to offer your clients. But always be prepared to counsel your clients as to what's possible given their budget. Present suitable alternatives no matter how large the purse may be, and you'll be substantiating your value from the start.

Knowing the Rituals

Many social events, especially religious celebrations, feature defined rituals that must be followed. Meetings with your clients will give you a sense of what they expect and how flexible they can be. Make sure to factor in additional time or staffing that will be necessary to meet their needs on the day of the event. In the case of a high Jewish wedding, one wedding planner shared with me her frustration at being asked at the last minute to incorporate many additional traditions into the wedding ceremony. You may wish to seek advice from an expert, such as a rabbi or priest, or ask your client to map out the day's activities in detail well in advance, including everything they'll need from you and your team.

Tapping into the Social Planning Market

After seeing the movie *The Wedding Planner,* who wouldn't want to don a headset and be the one racing around pulling all the pieces together for the most fabulous event of someone's lifetime? Unfortunately, while it looks glamorous, the steps from engagement until the bride and groom walk down the aisle are many and filled with oodles of details.

The first important detail of being a social planner is getting customers. Chapters 3 and 5 cover the development of your business and general marketing strategies. The social market offers some unique features and avenues for success, however, so here are some tips for breaking into this market.

- **Take out a specialized directory listing.** If you've held off on using your marketing dollars to take out a listing in the yellow pages, perhaps a very specific directory would be more beneficial and help you hit your target market. In my area there are several wedding guides listing lots of vendors who offer specialty services to wedding clients. These directories are available at bakeries, from caterers, and at venues that focus specifically on this clientele. While you would be one of many names, it will give you credibility and a presence in the marketplace.

Swim Before You Sink

Before you take your first project, go through a thorough checklist of the processes and make sure you're ready to go. Rely on your associates to support you in your weak areas. Do a dry run and walk through all the components of the social event so you're ready to be a valuable partner when your first client walks through the door.

- **Become a preferred vendor for facilities.** Most venues try to be as accommodating to their clients as possible. If they like you and feel you can enhance the wedding experience for their venue and their clients, they may allow you to become a preferred vendor. They will list you on their Web site, allow you to place brochures in their office or showroom, and suggest you to clients when asked. Some facilities may have requirements for being a preferred vendor, such as having a track record with them or producing a certain number of similar events.

- **Ask for referrals.** If you've enjoyed success with particular clients, they'll happily refer you to their friends and associates. Brides have sisters and friends getting married; couples have neighbors and family celebrating similar milestones. Don't be afraid to ask; you could be surprised at the leads you get.

- **Participate in local trade shows.** Many areas host specialized trade shows for social clients. Temples, hotels, and special venues often put on expositions or trade shows specializing in the wedding or bar mitzvah market. Check with your favorite vendors for advice on which shows in your area have reaped the best results.

- **Offer brochures at vendor shops and meetings.** Do some cold calling to your existing and potential vendors, asking if you can set out your brochures in their office. At professional meetings inquire about vendor display tables and ask to showcase at a monthly meeting. Once you develop these relationships, good vendors are happy to refer a reliable planner to clients.

The Challenges of Social Planning

- The events can be highly emotionally charged.
- You may have to deal with multiple managers—mother of bride, father of bride, bride. . . .
- There are almost certain to be budget constraints.
- You must have a thorough knowledge of event rituals.

- **Be seen and heard.** Once you become seasoned in your specialty area, write articles for local magazines on industry topics. Offer to speak on event-related issues in panels or at training sessions. If you know one aspect of the process well—catering or linens, for instance—you can stand out by strutting your stuff.

Social Planning Basics

The fundamental skill that any event planner brings to a client relationship is organization. Clients who hire a planner are looking for someone to pull all the details together. They need advice, organization, and attention to detail. Your main focus will be to show that you can meet your clients' needs for a successful outcome. Any social clients will look for these same skills, whether they're planning a wedding, bar or bat mitzvah, or birthday party. Your job is to use your natural skills in combination with your specialized training to make it happen!

What It Costs

Weddings, Bar and Bat Mitzvahs, Birthday Parties: $20–$3,000 per person based on the guest count, location, culinary selections, decor, and entertainment

Invitations: $1.00 and up based on personalization, calligrapher, and ribbon tying

Favors: $2.00–$200 based on item, engraving, materials

Entertainment: $400–$3,500+ DJ, $200+ live musicians per performer/hour, $1,200–$25,000+ band

Linens: $5.00–$50 rentals. $100+ for custom overlays and cloths

Florals: $20–$500+ for centerpieces, $75–$150+ for bouquets

Rentals: $5.00+ for tables, chairs, $.50+ for flatware, dishes, votives, decor

Photographer/Videographer: $1,200+

Lighting and Production Services: $2,500+

Tent Rentals: $3,000+

Limousine Services: $350+

Communication Skills

Even if you're the most organized and detail-oriented person in the world, if you can't communicate this to your clients to set their minds at ease, you won't have an easy relationship. While clients don't need to know every detail, such as the challenges you face in securing your vendors or negotiating pricing, or your frustrations in getting the necessary permits, they will make spot-check updates to be sure things are moving along. Remember that the reason they hired you was so that *you* could handle the details. Give them the end results but not every step that got you there. This will keep them comfortable that things are moving in a positive and forward direction, without growing overwhelmed by the process.

Creativity and Knowledge of Trends

Every planner has a responsibility to be aware of trends in the industry. If you're focusing on the social market, think in terms of children, brides, couples, families, and seasonal celebrations. Take the knowledge you gain about trends and put them in the creative context of the events you'll plan. Take the traditional, and factor in some untraditional. Use basic themes, and add the unexpected touches that show your clients they've hired a professional. By using your own creative juices, partnered with industry knowledge, you exemplify the value of a special event planner.

Knowledge of Risk Reduction and Legal Requirements

Another responsibility of a planner, social or otherwise, is knowledge of the latest requirements for legal and risk evaluation procedures. Planners must know how to limit risk and plan for safety throughout the event process. Good contracting will reduce your level of liability or place responsibility with the appropriate party, but the goal is to make sure legal action is never called for during one of your events. Knowledge, preplanning, and precautionary measures help ensure safe and trouble-free celebrations.

Wedding Party _____ Date _____

Planner:

Name: _____	Venue Location: _____
Information: _____	Information: _____
Cell: _____	Contact: _____
Phone: _____	Phone: _____
Fax: _____	Fax: _____
E-mail: _____	E-mail: _____

Thursday, June 7, 2007

9:00	Tent setup	Tent Company:
	Delivery of wine, supplies	Information:
	Easel, luminaries	Contact:
		Phone:
		Cell:
9:45	Planner arrives, lighting company arrives; oversee setup	Staff On Site: Contact Info:
6:15	Rehearsal	
7:30	Arrive at dinner location	Location:
8:00	Dinner	Contact Info:

Friday, June 8, 2007

9:00	Rental delivery: tables, chairs, linens	Vendor Info:
10:00		Contact Info:
11:00		
12:00	Setup of tables/linens/chairs	
1:00	Dress tent poles	
1:15	Set out ceremony chairs	
1:30	Set out luminaries	
3:00	Caterers arrive	
4:00	Florals delivered	
4:00	Photographer arrives	
4:15	Cake delivered	

4:30	Wedding party arrives, gets dressed, photos with bridesmaids
4:45	Musicians arrive
5:00	Judy goes to the hotel
5:00	Band arrives, starts setup
5:15	Justice of the peace arrives
5:30	Back upstairs
5:30	Trolley pickup at Viking
5:45	Trolley arrives at EH
6:00	Wedding begins
	Procession starts, runner is rolled down, bride proceeds
	JP conducts ceremony, B and G smooch, confetti is released, party begins
6:40	Cocktail hour/reception begins
	B and G take photos together on lawn
	Guests sign book and picture, get name/table cards
7:00	Catering captain invites guests to tent
7:30	Guests move into tent, dinner begins, first dance
7:40	Introductions of bride and groom into first dance
7:50	Toast, salad served
8:15	Entree served
	Music plays
	Band eats
8:50	Entree done, cut the cake, parents dance
9:30	Cake served, dessert buffet out
	Dancing continues
	Planner and staff depart
midnight	Dancing ends

Saturday, June 9, 2007

before	Decor removed
10:00 A.M.	Rental company picks up linens
	Lighting company removes lights

Knowledge of the Planning Process

Social clients will expect you not only to come up with the jazzy ideas, but also to make them happen. It takes timing and planning with the right team players to bring your greatest ideas to life. Everyone has to be on board, to know how his or her piece of the puzzle falls into place.

Develop a production schedule and share this with all your vendors. Let clients know when you'll begin setup and be ending your breakdown. Give them confidence that you have all the details in place.

Social Venues

Social clients will look to you to recommend and secure unique venues for their events. Make sure you keep your eyes open for unexpected spots to hold parties and gatherings. Be well versed in the capacity of your area's hotel ballrooms, country clubs, and reception halls, but also consider the unusual spots. Aquariums, historic buildings, barns, bowling alleys, museums, or private homes could offer just the right space for hosting an event. Or what about a park or boat? Some private areas are available for rental during the off-season or rent out their facilities for public functions only at specific times of year. Take a field trip to gather the details on venue options and keep them updated. Bringing the most interesting venue choices to your client could mean the difference between getting a project or not.

Decor Basics

One of the unique features of an event is its personality. A good planner will bring out the "event personality" through the theme development and

War Stories: No-Shows

In the very first wedding I planned, the musican ensemble scheduled to play during the ceremony failed to arrive. The bride had confirmed some of the details, and I confirmed others. This one element fell tragically through the cracks. When I realized the predicament (only ten minutes before the ceremony was to begin), I reacted promptly by asking the bandleader—the first of the band members to arrive—if he could possibly play recorded classical CD music during the procession. I had to let the bride know what was going on! I used humor and firmness to calm her: "The bad news is, the ensemble isn't here. The good news is, Mike is, and you're going to marry him in ten minutes." I quickly shared my proposed solution and assured her that the music would be appropriate. Luckily, the pianist arrived moments later and played a wonderful solo rendition of Pachelbel's *Canon* for the processional. The guests never realized that anything had been amiss, and the wedding continued without another hitch!

the creative use of decor. Here is just a sampling of areas where you can use your special touch to build the personality of the social event:

- **Tables.** Tablecloths, overlays, votives, confetti, petals, themed decorations
- **Centerpieces.** Tall, floral, unusual decorations
- **Lighting.** Room corners, outside and inside a tent, pin-spotting tables, table underlighting, special treatments for the buffet and band
- **Linens.** Dining, cocktail, reception, buffet, gift, cake, guest registration, guest book signing, and name card tables

jsmoran
1 Event Way
Celebrate, ON 54321

Invoice

DATE	INVOICE #
8/2/2007	001

Bill To
Bette Bride
123 Lovebird Lane
Celebration, ON 12345

P.O. NO.	TERMS	PROJECT
	due upon receipt	

QUANTITY	DESCRIPTION	RATE	AMOUNT
4	Hours of consulting services. Met with bride, discussed vendors and services, set appointments to meet with florist and linen companies.	75.00	300.00
100	Save-the-date cards: production and mailing services	10.00	1,000.00
Thank you for your business!		Total	$1,300.00

- **Placeware.** Chargers, plates (dinner, salad, dessert, bread), glasses (water, white wine, red wine, champagne), coffee cups, silverware
- **Room decor.** Props, lighting, effects (fog machine, gobos, lasers)
- **Tent decor.** Poles, tent entrances, sides
- **Favors.** Edible favors, donations, keepsakes, personalized gifts
- **Restrooms.** Flowers, potpourri, candles, amenity baskets, mints or other candies

By using your vendors and colleagues and staying up on the latest event trends, you'll create unique and memorable events for your social clients. Don't be afraid to think out of the box to create fresh looks. Start with the basic style of your clients and work to stretch them to the edge—but not out—of their comfort zones.

Weddings

One of the most exciting areas of social planning is weddings. Wedding planning provides an opportunity to specialize in an area of events that hold unique and varied characteristics. There are features of wedding planning that are driven by religious customs, nationality, budget, family expectations, age and background of the couple, colleges or universities attended, and of course style and personal preferences. Weddings can be small, intimate gatherings or lavish multiday events.

Destination Weddings

Destination weddings, ceremonies held in exotic or unusual locations away from the primary residence of the bride and groom, have become more and more popular. Many contemporary couples are professionals who have moved away from home for employment, have traveled and want to share their favorite destinations with family and friends, or who see the wedding as an opportunity for guests to enjoy an extended vacation while joining them in their special day. Typically destination weddings involve multi-events, from welcome receptions to gal and guy events. The rehearsal dinner can also be as elaborate or as time consuming as the reception as you create activities throughout the guests' stay. When budgeting your time for a destination wedding, be sure to list all the events you will be responsible for and price your services accordingly.

Becoming a wedding specialist requires you to know the nuances of the ceremony, the reception, and the religious or cultural beliefs that are important to your client. It will also demand you work carefully with all parties—family and friends included—to meet your client's expectations and deliver as stress-free a day as possible. Your services also may include being a resource for attire, invitations, favors, gift baskets, and other personalized items that the couple will want to include. Your list of vendors to support these requests will also grow as you are asked to assist your client in the various details of the wedding process. Don't be afraid to call in the pros, such as a graphic designer or personal stylist if the bride's expectations warrant it. Just update your budget and give the couple options to select the level of service and price that they are comfortable with.

Frequently Asked Questions

I received a call from a bride-to-be to assist with the wedding. But when I met with the client and her mom, I got the clear impression that the mother of the bride would be doing most of the planning. How do I proceed with my client without getting anyone upset, especially myself?

It is often a delicate balance to satisfy both a bride who is feeling overwhelmed with the planning of her special day and is asking for professional assistance and the mother of the bride who has waited a lifetime to create a magical day for her daughter. This is when you must listen, be tactful, and put it in writing. Try to get a commitment on the scope of your relationship from the start so you aren't spinning your wheels to develop theme ideas and concepts that ultimately won't be received with open arms. Incorporate the ideas from the mom and bride with your experience in execution so you create a win-win for everyone. But don't try to sell them on something they do not want—if they want tulle, let them do tulle, but guide them toward ways to take a fresh approach.

I really love children and think I could offer great ideas for parties and favors. How do I make money at it?

For children's parties, think in terms of simplicity and numbers. You may not be doing lavish floral arrangements, but if you develop a decor package that you can personalize for different themes and is at the right price-point, you may hit the mark. For a children's party itemize the elements that are critical—theme, table decor, favors, and games—and produce an array of these for clients to pick from to do their one-stop shopping. It will save parents time in putting together all the details, and once you have the system in place, it will take you little time to execute!

I provided my client with a list of services I can provide and charge on a percentage. Now she is going directly to vendors that are the higher-priced elements of the event and having me do the items that I make the least amount of money on! How can I get paid for my ideas and vendor contacts?

It's hard to make an exciting pitch for an event without giving too much information away. I would suggest you talk in "wide brushstrokes" and not get into the finer details of how to execute. Don't give away your resources either. Keep your vendor list close to your chest. If a trusted vendor gets a call directly from a client, they could always provide you with a finder's fee, or direct the client back to you for contracting and production planning. Let your vendors know you are thinking of using them for an upcoming event and clear the date with them beforehand. Give the client's name, and work out how they will handle any direct contact.

What other services could I provide to enhance my social event business?

Try providing home decorating for parties—table accent items, ideas on theming for in-home parties or holidays. Stationery items such as invitations or announcements are also a good way to round out services you can offer to your social clients. You may consider offering gift items such as welcome baskets or party favors. Think of the accoutrements to the party, from favors to decorations, and try to find a niche that you can showcase your services with.

10 Corporate Events

The corporate event market offers a variety of planning opportunities. If you enjoy a more businesslike approach to special events, the corporate client is a good match for you. If you think in terms of strategic development, measurability of event goals and objectives, and accountability, you'll be on the same wavelength when meeting with a corporate client. Even if your client isn't bringing up these topics, such issues will be the heart and soul of the corporate event and should be the driving force behind your planning techniques. The corporate client is more foundation than fluff, more process that parade, more results driven than emotion driven.

The Various Corporate Events

If you're working with a marketing department, you may see product launches, sales promotion events, or trade-show-related events. These tend to be in various locations, based on the industry exhibit schedule or the company's target market. The attendees will be customers, existing or potential, that your clients would like an audience with. Special events are perfect vehicles for promoting goodwill between customer and client and allow sales and executive staff to get to know their business partners on a more casual and friendly basis.

The human resource department will handle employee-related events such as award dinners, holiday outings, team-building events, training programs, summer outings, or incentive events. They can be held at or near the company headquarters or at a location chosen for its exclusivity to serve as a reward for sales or superior efforts within the company.

Types of Corporate Events

- Product launches
- Conferences and meetings
- Sales events
- Customer appreciation events
- Team building
- Employee training
- Anniversary events
- Award dinners
- Incentive events
- Trade-show-related events
- Retirement parties
- Holiday outings
- Summer outings
- Ground-breaking ceremonies
- Ribbon-cuttings or grand openings

A CEO may drive the arrangements for a corporate anniversary celebration or retirement event for a high-level officer. You may deal directly with the executive, his or her administrative assistant, or the board of directors. As an outside planner, you can be a valuable resource to small and midsized companies in many ways. Once you get your foot in the door, explore opportunities to offer your planning services to other departments.

Familiarize Yourself with Your Clients

Before the planning of a corporate event begins, you should familiarize yourself with the corporate culture. In chapter 8, I covered the elements of a proposal and questions to ask in order to plan an appropriate event, but there are other areas to be aware of when managing a corporate event. Knowing your audience and the goals of the event will allow you to recommend the best elements that fit for your client.

If you'll be dealing with a mostly male crowd and spouses aren't invited, don't plan on a dance band. If you have a high percentage of attendees who prefer vegetarian meals, don't plan a filet mignon entree. Choose event elements that match the profile and expectations of the host. By thoroughly investigating the background of your group, it will help ensure success on the day or evening of the event!

It's critical to discuss certain event components with corporate clients very early in the planning process. These include the time span for serving alcohol, the monitoring of alcohol consumption, the handling of after-parties, and liability issues. It's important to advise your clients on the ethical and legal implications of the decisions they make in these areas. In some situations certain behavior may be more acceptable, but this could still invite disaster if implemented at a corporate-sponsored event. As a planner you are responsible for achieving the best outcome for the event, and it's important to cover all bases to protect yourself, your clients, and the attendees.

Nuances of the Corporate Client

Unlike the social client, who tends to rule with the heart, the corporate client rules more by the wallet. Most events revolve around driving the success of their business. Sales events, award dinners, and trade show events are held for the ultimate purpose of improving the bottom line. I don't mean, by the way, to paint a picture of misdirected values—the goals of making a profit and running a successful business are valid. Indeed, chances are that you share them in your own home-based enterprise! Successful companies hire workers, drive a strong economy, and keep the wheels of commerce running strong. And events, which provide a unique opportunity for interaction within the business setting, are essential vehicles in bolstering business success.

Corporate clients will look for professional methods in the event development process. While they may not need to know all the details of the planning, they will want to be kept abreast of changes to your proposal or contract that affect the event outcome or pricing. They'll let you choose the color of the flowers, but they'll want to make sure you've been thoughtful about the decor and will want to see your recommendations. The social client, on the other hand, is often more of a micromanager, wanting to choose the flowers, the vases, and the way they're placed on the table to complement the room or attire of the hostess. The corporate client is more hands-off with the details but more demanding on results. If an event does not achieve the desired objectives, its life cycle will be relatively short. Most events have natural life cycles that range from three to seven years. Companies look for fresh approaches, and if you aren't acting as their creative consultant developing new vehicles to

> ### Corporate Event Checklist
>
> - What type of event is planned?
> - What are the purpose and goals for the event?
> - What is the guest profile? Age, background, ethnicity?
> - What is the ratio of male to female?
> - Will spouses be involved?
> - What is the time of event—evening, day, during work, at a conference?
> - What is the mix of management and staff?
> - Are there any health or physical restrictions?
> - Are there any security issues or concerns?
> - How many host executives will be attending?
> - Will they have any special needs, such as speeches or travel arrangements?
> - What key clients will be attending?
> - What host staff members will be attending?
> - What evaluation methods are desired?

meet their goals, you'll be out of a client in a matter of time.

In a corporate relationship you'll typically be working with a manager such as a human resource director for employee events, a marketing director for sales and marketing events, or perhaps a CEO for companywide events or in the case of a small business. The closer you are to the top, in terms of your relationship with the client, the better: It means fewer channels to go through for approval, less chance of confusion over goals, expectations, and budget, and less hands-on involvement in the process of planning by the client. Most executives choose a planner because they see the value of selecting an expert to do a job they themselves are not prepared to undertake.

One challenge of relationships with corporate clients is the changing of the guard. When decision makers change, they often bring a new support team in with them. They may have prior relationships that they feel obligated to honor or are more comfortable with. Through no fault of your own, then, you can be easily replaced when new executives come in and bring their favorite planner on board with them.

Do stay in touch with transferred executives, however, because you may be able to pick up event projects at their new place of business. Indeed, if you do your job well you'll find that the relationships you've begun often extend beyond the workplace. I've made many lasting friendships as a result of working closely with clients on events. Events are very personal, and because you give so much of yourself in the process, you touch people's lives on a much deeper level than with most jobs. To me that is one of the most rewarding parts of event planning!

The way information concerning the event is disseminated and managed is quite different for the corporate event planner. Social events have

invitations; corporate events may have internal news releases or flyers or may involve the public relations or corporate communications department. You may have nothing to do with this dissemination, or you may be asked to do it all. You might be able to offer suggestions to tie in your theme from the very beginning by offering to manage the invitation or announcement design and production.

If clients are interested in getting press coverage for an event, you may want to team up with someone experienced with the media to write press releases, develop a press kit, and manage follow-up with press agencies. Bringing in the media involves a specific process, so you'd be wise to familiarize yourself with it, or outsource it.

Small clients may request that you develop announcements and manage the database of responses. This can be easily done with a good database management program. With fax and e-mail blasts, planned follow-up with invitees can help drive up attendance percentages. Once again, if you cannot manage this yourself, hire someone to help—another way you can add value to your client relationship.

Working on a corporate project calls for strong written and verbal communication skills and the ability to work both independently and as a team member. Depending on the scope of the event and the size of the company, many tiers of the organization could be involved—all of which need information on the event planning process. Or you may find that once the budget is approved, clients want to do nothing more than arrive at the event and enjoy the festivities. Because you must handle

What It Costs

Proposal Development: $25–$1,200 (laptop presentation with photos to full diagram, schematic,
and model prototype)

Incentives: $15–$150 (cards, logo incentives,
wearables for staff/client gifts)

Specialized Invitations: $15–$150+ per invitation,
including mailing costs

all styles of leadership and corporate management, you'll need systems in place to deliver with
ease. Use complete timelines and production
schedules to drive the planning process, and keep
your budgets up to date and accurate. (Refer back
to the sample timelines and production schedules
in chapter 8.) Be able to answer the treasurer's
questions as well as those from the marketing
director. You'll want to keep everyone who's
involved comfortable and informed during the
planning process.

Events at Trade Shows

Corporate exhibitors are always interested in
ways to stretch their exhibition dollars by making
the most of the trade show experience. Receptions and hospitality events may be held at
hotels, off-site venues, and unique locations to
increase attendance. Smaller events offer more
one-on-one opportunities with sales/executive
staff and clients; larger events, such as international galas, allow for sales staff and executives
to entertain many guests in one location rather
than traveling worldwide for sales calls. This
strategy covers enormous ground considering
transportation cost and travel time for sales staff.

As a planner, you can assist with corporate-
hosted dinner events. Block off premier restaurants for sales staff to entertain clients. This gives
a salesperson attending the show the opportunity to book a luncheon or dinner with customers
either in advance or at the last minute.

Announcements or Invitations

Begin the event introduction with newsletter-
style print pieces that cover the upcoming show,
city highlights, industry news, company info, and
service profiles. Send them out well in advance of
the show. Follow up quarterly to keep your
clients' name in front of customers.

An event invitation can range from a specialty
hand-designed three-dimensional boxed piece
that creates a sense of mystery and excitement
about the upcoming event, to a high-end item
such as a bottle of wine for an excursion to a vine-
yard. For a more economical invitation, try a fax or
e-mail version with clip art and the event basics.
(Note, however, that many businesses are becoming averse to downloading attached files due to
the possibility of contracting computer viruses.
Creating PDF files or enlisting a Web-based invitation service can help facilitate this process.)

Follow-up is essential, preferably by salespeo-
ple who personally know the invited guests. If the
list is large and doesn't allow for this, follow-up
faxes or e-mails can elicit responses and help
drive strong attendance.

The Event

An off-site event at a trade show will stretch the face-to-face time your clients have with customers. If they're looking for broad coverage, try to hire name entertainers to lure in the crowd. If quality, not quantity, is what they're going for, select a site that represents the city they're visiting and theme it up as Southwest, nautical, or sports. Or base the theme on the venue they select—perhaps a winery, aquarium, or museum. Go for the unusual and layer another theme on, such as Moulin Rouge, Hooray for Hollywood, the 1950s (or 1960s, or 1970s), Beatle Mania, Space Odyssey, or the like to create a fun environment.

Forgo the props and hit them with sound, lighting, and stretch fabrics for a contemporary look. Don't forget to pack in the entertainment. Offer something to everyone. A mix of stationary and moving musicians will keep the evening dynamic. A high point should always be planned for the close of the event. This will leave folks with a lasting memory and keep them eager to receive next year's invitation.

Food services should complement the theme. Complete themed menu suggestions are available through members of professional organizations such as the National Association of Catering Executives. This can help you create extraordinary and trendy selections and provide your guests with a unique dining experience.

Evaluation

Make use of the information your corporate clients have on their booth attendees and invited

War Stories: Dove Soup, Anyone?

A corporate planner, trying to pull a memorable "Wow," scheduled a dramatic dove drop during a convention center ballroom luncheon event. He planned for everything, it seemed . . . except the very warm weather. When the dove nets were opened, hundreds of expired birds dropped suddenly to the beautiful tables below. Guests got more than they ordered at that event!

A word to the wise: Consider the environment you're working in and the props you'll be using. Think through all the pros and cons and balance the risk of failure against the benefit of success.

guests. Track their sales activities, hosted events, and exhibit experience for solid quantitative information on the benefits. Use the database for follow-up mailings containing post-exhibit or post-event news.

Track not only direct increases in sales, but leads generated from these clients or their willingness to see the sales staff after the event date or listen to product updates. Compare sales generated following the event to sales during similar periods with no marketing event activities. Although this may not be an "apples-to-apples" comparison—market conditions, competition, and a variety of other factors can all influence the outcome—it could offer an interesting and valuable perspective.

At some level, the goodwill and strengthening of relationships that come from a successful event can provide clients with a long-term benefit not easily reduced to a percentage or number on a chart. By using both qualitative and quantitative evaluations, you can enhance your clients' understanding of the value of their events.

Current Trends in Corporate Events

Corporate strategists are always looking for ways to deliver their key messages, and events can provide a powerful outlet if care is taken to understand corporate objectives and thread these into all aspects of your event delivery. Many event planners are using integrated programming—scaling back to one core concept, and integrating this into all aspects of their event. From premiums to speakers to programming, every element of the event reinforces one message to achieve a seamless implementation of the corporate objective. Your corporate clients will call on you to present their chosen theme throughout all the event elements. Be organized and creative. Don't be afraid to share your challenges with your vendors. They may be able to offer ideas on how their product or services could be incorporated to meet your clients' goals.

Get to Know Your Audience

One planner I know responds to her clients' needs by fitting the right entertainment into corporate events. It's a good strategy: Use an entertainment company that has access to top national headline entertainers to deliver hot acts that draw attendees to events. If the budget allows and you can bring a popular act into an intimate setting, it's a draw. People won't want to miss seeing Tina Turner or the Rolling Stones at a small venue . . . it's a once-in-a-lifetime opportunity to get up close to a celebrity, with the added benefit of photo ops and autograph sessions. By researching what drives your attendees—their ages and demographics—you can increase your chances for a strong turnout by showcasing the right artists.

Consider your audience's socioeconomic mix, the male–female ratio, international representation, and corporate culture. All these factors should drive your suggestions for music (an older group may not appreciate rap, or a younger crowd a classical ensemble); food (some cultures might not enjoy certain cuisine, so offer variety—and always a vegetarian option); and decor (don't make it too wild for a reserved group; get advice from the internal planning committee).

Pack a Punch with Technology and Imagery

The best in tech is still the way to stay on the edge of design and decor. A specialty production company can help you find ways to stay within tight budgets by pairing a state-of-the-art lighting and video entertainment package with more traditional fabric backdrops to create dynamic event environments. All the lights, camera, music, and action can be softened with high-quality painted fabric to tie in with any themed event. Backdrop companies offer images ranging from African safaris and Moroccan villages to fantasy, western, or city skylines; these can turn an ordinary hotel ballroom from simple to spectacular in a few hours.

jsmoran

1 Event Way

Celebrate, ON 54321

Invoice

DATE	INVOICE #
8/2/2007	client 02

Bill To
Mr. John Smith
Corporate Client
One Financial Way
Profit, CT

DESCRIPTION	AMOUNT
10 hours of consulting services. Event planning and management services for Employee Awards Dinner, meetings to discuss progress, presentation of award options, update on vendors and event progress, ongoing management of vendors	$1,000.00
300 award plaques personalized	4,500.00
Thank you for your business!	Total $5,500.00

Create a Well-Oiled Machine

Developing a strong network of professional vendors should become an essential part of your business plan. They will help you bring the latest and greatest with the greatest of ease to any event. At one company outing, I called on my event colleagues from the International Special Events Society to create an interactive circus experience for the participants. Members of ISES New England were pulled together to bring their talents to the table for a day of hands-on fun for the 200 attendees.

Guests enjoyed trying their hand at juggling, plate spinning, and tightrope walking. Artists performed throughout the day, culminating in a multiperformer grand finale show under the big top. An interactive DJ laid down background music interspersed with fun games and contests. The event ran smoothly because these pros knew what was expected of them—and what to expect of each other—and worked together as a team. I have duplicated this experience with a formal gala. No matter what the situation, the right team will help you create a stress-free event.

Selecting the right combination of elements for successful corporate event planning is continually redefined, minute by minute and project by project. You must be aware of tightened budgets, more stringent evaluation measures, and a company's constant need to validate the expense and time spent on the event process. Think of it as a challenge—a way to stay on your event planning toes!

Frequently Asked Questions

Where can I get ideas for corporate clients to deliver events that really hit the mark?

Listening to your clients is the first step. Give them what they really want, not what is in vogue or you are dying to try out. If you have a client that is looking for out-of-the-box ideas for their events, try attending a regional or national event trade show or conference that offers exhibits and state-of-the-art showcases so you can stay up on the latest products and services available.

When coordinating an off-site event, how many planning trips should I make beforehand?

It depends if you are using a reputable local resource to assist you and how far away it is located. You should certainly make a preview trip to interview local vendors that you will use and preview locations. Try to schedule any tastings or walk-throughs at venues as well. Things like demo tapes or schematics for room layouts can be sent or e-mailed as the project unfolds. If you have a reliable local company or planner, you may only need one trip. Try to arrive several days in advance before the event to work out any last-minute details.

How can I tap into business events in my small town?

Join a local chamber of commerce to get to know your business community. Consider doing grand openings or auto dealership events that need decor/balloons or catering support. Try to assist in marketing efforts at banks. Take out an advertisement or sponsor a sports team by getting a listing in their program booklet. Eventually your company name will get around as a resource for event planning.

Where is the best place to start to get business in corporate events?

Depending on the area you want to specialize in, you may start with Human Resources for company outings, Marketing Department for sales incentive events or trade-show-related events, or Investor Relations for grand openings and community outreach events. In a small company you may even work directly with an owner or his or her administrative assistant to help with special events.

11

Nonprofit and Fund-Raising Events

The nonprofit segment of the event planning field offers a wide variety of opportunities. Many professionals get their start working as volunteers on town-sponsored events, school fund-raisers, or citywide health fairs and activities. Besides the satisfaction of working on an exciting event, the altruistic elements of a fund-raising project can also be very rewarding.

Getting Your Foot in the Door

Because the goal of a fund-raiser is to raise money for a not-for-profit organization, the tendency is for these clients to be very cautious about the ratio of expenses to income. For this reason developing a relationship with nonprofits is very different from the process involved with social or corporate clients. Many large groups have paid staff in place who manage their special events. Other organizations look for volunteers to handle details and may sometimes hire a few key professionals to oversee areas that they're unfamiliar with. Small local organizations—say, school or church groups—may be used to relying totally on volunteers and may not embrace the expense of a professional planner.

One way to get started in this area of event planning is to offer your services as a sponsor. You may charge event elements such as decor, rentals, or catering at cost, or offer to pass on any volume discounts you receive directly to the group. You could donate your planning skills as an event sponsor. In exchange, you should request visibility for your company in the invitation, the program booklet, or the event's signage. Depending on the event, you could gain access to many prestigious attendees, who'll see your work and perhaps call you for more lucrative projects.

Consulting to Nonprofits

When working with a nonprofit, you should clearly define the event goals. Typically, you'll be reporting to a board of directors that makes decisions for the group. In initial meetings with a board, you should determine the level of support for a special event and make sure the members embrace this as the answer to their fund-raising or capital campaign goals. (Efforts to raise the major funds that cover a group's operating expenses are often referred to as *capital campaigns*.)

A key donor who's interested in holding a celebratory event may hire you to oversee the planning. Even in this situation, the board has the ultimate decision-making power, and you should

seek its support and approval. The board may ultimately decide to use the donor's funds for operating expenses and forgo the event. This has happened to me in the past. Despite all my efforts to educate the group about all the positive results an event could bring—gathering new donors into the fold, creating esprit de corps in the community, spreading out the donor base to include more than one major contributor—the board chose to pass up the large gala. Fortunately, I was compensated for my planning time up to that point and will hopefully have an opportunity to work with the group on future events.

As a professional planner, you can help your nonprofit clients develop a plan for incorporating special events into their fund-raising and capital campaign efforts. You can educate them as to the advantages of special events, as well as the planning process such events entail. Mary Beth Miller, a seasoned event pro, shared some ideas on educating the nonprofit client during a fund-raising basics course and developed the core elements of a planning tool that I now use. The questionnaire and project overview you'll see on page 135 helps me walk my clients through the planning process; forces them to make decisions on the scope of the project; and addresses some critical issues.

Nonprofit Event Basics

The same basic elements make up a nonprofit event as any other. Theme, decor, cuisine, and so on should all partner with the goals of the organization. Whether it's a fun walk or a black-tie gala, the planning will start with the theme of the

Nonprofit Opportunities

- Medical or health causes
- Environmental groups
- Children or family organizations
- Museums
- Religious organizations
- Schools, universities, and colleges
- Hospitals
- Human service agencies
- State or government groups

Nonprofit Service Questionnaire and Project Overview

Purpose of event:

- What are the financial goals and other goals of the event?
- What is the overall theme or underlying force driving the event?
- What is the attendance goal and mix?
- What are the sponsorship goals?
- What promotional activities will be planned?

Ownership of event:

- Who are the directors, leaders, and/or committee members?
- What will the roles or chain of command be?
- What are the responsibilities of the nonprofit board and of the event planner? Will the planner attend every management, staff, or planning meeting? If so, how many such meetings will there be?
- Who manages accountability?
- How will recognition of achievement be handled for committee volunteers?
- What is the volunteer-to-paid-staff ratio for the nonprofit?

Expectations:

- What are the sales, sponsorship, and donor projections for the event?
- What net proceeds are expected?
- What's the budget of income and expenses? The organization's financial commitment?
- What are the contingency plans and priority lists for the event?

Management policies and provisions:

- What legal policies and provisions are in place?
- Tax policies and provisions?
- Insurance?
- Accounting?

Database management:

- Is an initial guest list available? How will it be updated?
- Is a target list of donor and attendees available?
- What will the registration process be?
- The follow-up procedure?

Nonprofit Service Questionnaire (continued)

Event scripting:

- How will the production schedule for the actual event be coordinated?
- Are contingency plans and outcome variables available?
- Who will manage staff? Is a duty outline available?
- What are the roles and responsibilities of the volunteer staff?

Event evaluation:

- What is the measure of success from board, guests, sponsors, donors, volunteers?
- What would we change (if anything!) for next year?

campaign and include all the elements supporting it. Announcements, public relations involvement, site selection, entertainment, and safety measures—all the familiar planning components should be factored in.

Meeting Financial Goals

Working with nonprofits has some special features, however. Unique elements of a fund-raising event include silent auctions and sponsorships. Engaging key donors to support ticket sales and to offer product and services for auctioning is crucial. Key event sponsors receive publicity in programs distributed at the event, on the event's signs, and so on. There also may be levels of visibility, based on sponsorship levels. When budgeting with a board, I often present scenarios comparing funds raised with combinations of ticket sales and sponsorship or auction dollars. This helps my clients set goals and focus on results.

Gaining exposure for the event may also be a key objective for the board. Reaching out into the community, getting local media coverage, or even holding a press conference to create excitement about the event can all increase the group's visibility and, ultimately, its public support. As a planner you may not want to assume responsibility for this role; it may be more appropriate to draw on the board's publicity staff and experience or on a professional public relations person.

Working with a Board

The key to putting on successful fund-raising events for nonprofits is a strong advisory board and/or sponsor. Along with a working board, or board of directors, comes the nonprofit's advisory or honorary board. Members are usually key community figures who embrace the mission of the nonprofit and have the desire and ability to drive results. Their names should be visible on any print

School Fund-Raising Options

Fund-Raising Event

Scenario One: 50 couples attend/50 families attend

Revenue	#	Cost per	Total
Ticket sales	50 @	$ 1,000	$ 50,000
Family ticket sales	50 @	$ 10	$ 500
Raffle proceeds			$ 1,000
Silent auction proceeds			$ 20,000
Live auction proceeds			$ 10,000
Sponsorship donation			$ 33,000
Income			$ 114,500
Expenses			
F&B—couple	100 @	$ 200	$ 20,000
F&B—families	150 @	$ 30	$ 4,500
Entertainment: ensemble, soloist, magician, performance artists			$ 4,000
Invitations			$ 1,000
Decor, signage, banners			$ 5,000
Planning services			$ 10,000
Expenses			$ 44,500
Balance to school			$ 70,000

Fund-Raising Event

Scenario Two: 100 couples attend/100 families attend

Revenue	#	Cost per	Total
Ticket sales	100 @	$ 1,000	$ 100,000
Family ticket sales	100 @	$ 10	$ 1,000
Raffle proceeds			$ 3,000
Silent auction proceeds			$ 30,000
Live auction proceeds			$ 10,000
Sponsorship donation			
Income			$ 144,000
Expenses			
F&B—couple	200 @	$ 200	$ 40,000
F&B—families	400 @	$ 30	$ 12,000
Entertainment: ensemble, soloist, magician, performance artists			$ 4,000
Invitations			$ 3,000
Decor, signage, banners			$ 5,000
Planning services			$ 10,000
Expenses			$ 74,000
Balance to school			$ 70,000

What It Costs

Keynote Speaker/Celebrity: $2,000+

Auctioneer: 3 percent to 10 percent of sales

Auction Software: $250+

material that identifies the event. Members of the advisory board typically don't participate in planning or working meetings but rather offer their prestige in the community to drive ticket sales and auction success.

Managing Volunteers

Nonprofit events often engage large numbers of volunteers. While this of course keeps staffing expenses low, it also calls for more training and management work on your part. Volunteers will be needed for greeting guests and managing on-site activities. You'll want to schedule training sessions to equip these volunteers with the information they need to carry out the goals and objectives of the board. Besides a passion for the nonprofit and enthusiasm for special events, they'll need clear direction and specific duties to keep things running smoothly. Expect to find a wide assortment of abilities and knowledge in the group, and start with the basics of proper event execution to put everyone on the same page. Develop a clear organizational chart, with specific lines of command and procedures in case of emergency or if contin-

gency plans kick in. Don't let volunteers bear the responsibility of making final decisions on important issues. Let them know who to report to in all situations.

You'll use all your basic planning tools and procedures—timelines, production schedules, vendor agreements and contracts—with a fundraising event. The larger the effort, the more important the attention to detail becomes. If you're working on a citywide fun run or walk, for instance, safety measures and licensing or permitting must be in place. For a carnival or children's event, consider the unique precautions necessary for safe execution, such as medical stations, help desks, and lost-and-found areas. Plan for a police detail, if necessary, or on-site medical personnel. Be sure to discuss your insurance requirements with your board and make sure you or they are appropriately covered.

Celebrity Appearances

Everyone loves a celebrity—and that includes nonprofits. There may be no easier way to pump up event attendance and proceeds than to book a star appearance. Sometimes celebrities can be secured for little or no cost through personal or professional relationships. Whether you pay for a celebrity or are lucky enough to garner one pro bono, here are some suggestions to make the process run smoothly!

Selecting the Appropriate Celebrity

Begin by examining your target audience. What are the ages, expectations, and interests of your group? Would a sports figure, local politician, or

Checklist for Choosing a Celebrity

- What's the profile of the target donors (age, expectations, interests)?
- What's the event theme?
- What's the capital campaign theme?
- Where will the event take place?
- What's the nonprofit's message?
- What's the budget?
- Do any board members have existing relationships with suitable celebrities?
- Are there any sponsor relationships that would be advantageous?

or sponsors may have existing relationships that allow you to secure a celebrity for little or even nothing. You'd be surprised at who knows whom, or whose relative is the next-door neighbor of such-and-such movie star or sports hero. Ask and you just may receive!

As a good planner, you'll want to be hospitable to your celebrity guests as well as making sure you're well versed with their personal requirements. Depending on their level of renown, they may need security, limousine service, hotel accommodations, or even airfare if they're coming in from out of the area. Inform

movie star be the most exciting draw for your event? What public figure might best complement the nonprofit's campaign theme, and your own event theme?

Depending on the location of your event, you may have access to suitable celebrities who live locally, thus eliminating or reducing your transportation and lodging expenses. Brainstorm with your board to generate a list of people passionate about the nonprofit's message. There may be a local author, war hero, politician, or educator who can offer support for the health, education, social, or environmental cause that your group embraces.

Although you will always want to work within your group's budget to select the appropriate charismatic figure for your event, board members

Celebrity Requirements Checklist

- Security
- Travel arrangements
- Transportation at destination
- Transportation to and from event
- Accommodations
- Hospitality arrangements—suite, incidental gift, floral and food arrangements
- Briefing booklet—details of celebrities' activities, timeline, important contact information
- Special requirements—dietary, physical, additional security
- On-site coordination—staff assistance, security, press assistance

The Celebrity's Contract

Even if celebrities agree to appear at your fundraising event for free, it's a good idea to draw up a contract formalizing everyone's needs and expectations. Will you want them to sign autographs, have photos taken with key members or guests, have their name in the paper and identified with your group and the event? Don't forget, celebrities may already be working under an agency contract that limits their exposure. Ask about this from the start rather than risk disappointment on the day of the event.

You'll want to make sure all of the following are spelled out in writing in any contract with a celebrity:

- **Fees.** Spell out monetary arrangements clearly. Will a board member arrange for a complimentary appearance? Will you work through a speaker bureau or entertainment agency? Get everything in writing.
- **Celebrity requirements.** Discuss these fully, and document them for clarity.
- **Nonprofit expectations.** Think about the length of the visit, autograph signing, photos, a VIP reception, audience, and so forth.

Publicity

Good public relations can help you get maximum mileage out of your celebrity appearance. Publicity decisions will be governed by your target audience, of course, as well as by your budget and the approval and support of your board.

What kinds of publicity options do you have? Think about the following:

- Develop a press kit to send to key contacts in print and broadcast media.
- Host a VIP reception allowing the nonprofit's top donors to meet the celebrity face to face.
- Make a general announcement in newspapers or local, national, or industry publications.
- Advertise on radio or television for the widest possible reach.

How you time your information release can be a critical factor in getting the message across. You can make the initial announcement when the celebrity contract is signed and the date and event are confirmed. Plan on staggering your follow-up publicity for the most effective delivery. Again, think about your target market, the number of attendees you're looking to draw, the exclusivity of the appearance, and the price tag for attendance. If you'll be charging $500 per ticket for a VIP reception, for instance, you might want to send an elegant invitation to the nonprofit's top donors. Once again, a strong advisory board is critical to put this list of key people together.

Also consider whether the celebrity visit can be linked to such current events as book releases,

your staff of the details of the visit, including pertinent phone numbers and contact information. You might wish to include a small gift or welcoming basket or flowers as part of your greeting. Special needs such as food limitations or medical care should be addressed as well.

movie premieres, social or cultural achievements, and so on. These may create opportunities for autograph or photo sessions, keynote messages, or event theme tie-ins. Would other activities such as visits to schools, hospitals, libraries, or civic centers be appropriate?

Auction Basics

Most nonprofits include fund-raising in their special event game plan. Both live and silent auctions play a big part in generating income and contributions. Soliciting gift auction items and coordinating packaging, display, and print support help to create interest, excitement, and ultimately donations for the nonprofit organization. Make sure you have a strong network of volunteer support to assist with sponsorship, auction solicitation, ticket sales, decorating and setup, registration, closeout, checkout, and cleanup. Even sending thank-you notes and asking for participation in next year's event are important duties to assign to volunteer helpers.

When setting up your auction items, take time to package them in an attractive way. Bundle single donations together into a "gift pack" to increase bidding prices. Lay the items out in an organized way in your program booklet, and arrange them on decorated tables with signage and bid sheets that will list bidders' numbers and bid prices. Try not to burn volunteers or donors out by asking too much or too often. While it can be exciting to create a high-end charity event at a country club or hotel, watch the costs that go into

room rentals and food minimums. Your guests may be just as happy at a local restaurant snacking on cocktails and hors d'oeuvres and mingling around the auction tables rather than dining on a plated dinner and stuck at an assigned table all night. As long as you spell out the purpose, attire, and event parameters, most guests are happy to attend to contribute to a reputable charity.

Items to Include in a Silent or Live Auction

- Trips, including accommodations, airfare, and stipends, ranging from weekends to full weeks. Destinations can be a country home, exotic island, ski resort, or warm-weather bungalow.
- Beauty or spa items, including products, services, clothing, or travel packages.
- Sporting events and packages that include equipment, signed memorabilia, or event tickets.
- Artwork (can be personalized for bidder).
- Photography.
- Art, music, or theater event tickets.
- Home services, including cleaning, repair, automotive.
- Lessons—music, sporting, art, photography, language, tutoring.
- Large items such as pianos, automobiles, televisions, or video/music equipment.
- Purebred pets or pet training services.
- Priceless items, such as lunch with a principal, lesson with a pro.

War Stories: Preparation Is Key

Prepping a celebrity for a speaking engagement can be as important as hiring one. At one event where a young man was presenting a motivational speech to middle school students, not enough attention was paid to preparing him for his presentation in front of such a large audience. Although he had started his own foundation for children of cancer victims during his high school years, had made key appearances on national TV during college, and had been hired by a major corporation as a spokesperson, he was not prepared to deliver an eloquent and meaningful speech to the youngsters. This event might have run much more smoothly if planners had helped him review his material, giving him suggestions on timing, delivery, and the kinds of questions he could expect from the audience.

Working with not-for-profit groups can be both exciting and rewarding—not to mention offering a strong business base for the special event planner. A wide variety of fund-raising organizations—schools, communities, medical and health organizations, and church, religious, and family groups—may all host events that range from galas to parades, fairs to fetes. You'll have the opportunity to expand your skills as you work with volunteers, boards of directors, and new and existing vendors; you'll also be pushed to stretch your management skills, planning abilities, and decor dollars. All this, plus the chance to raise money for a wonderful cause, make nonprofit events well worth the challenges along the way!

Frequently Asked Questions

My client wants a big-name celebrity to attend to drive ticket sales. How can I make this happen?

Start with your advisory board to see who has connections to secure a big-name star. Many advisory members can pull in a favor or brainstorm to find out who knows whom. This is the easiest and least expensive way to approach celebrity appearances. The second approach would be to contact a speaker's bureau and contract the celebrity for a fee. Fees will include time, travel, and other expenses. And don't forget the hospitality items you will want to plan to make your celebrity guest comfortable.

I am coordinating a school fund-raiser. Do I need to get permitting or licenses to sell food or have any amusements?

Treat a fund-raising event like any other event and cover all bases. Check with your school on their policies on food preparation and sales. Follow through to local agencies concerning taxes, permits, and licenses. Don't forget tenting and rain dates if it is an outside event. Consider safety features such as help desks, EMTs, or nurse stations. Depending on the location of the event, activities, and the expected ages and attendee numbers, an on-call ambulance service may make sense as well.

Is it possible for me to not charge for my services and take a cut of the proceeds?

Anything is possible, but the success of the event and donations will depend on the type of event, the history of donations, the current economic situation, what other events you may be competing with, and the strength of the advisory board to drive attendance and donations. You will also have to look at your ability to execute and "sell" the event. I would recommend doing your homework and starting slow with commitments to the nonprofit to ensure you cover your labor, time, and materials.

I have volunteered for years and want to get paid for my time in coordinating fund-raising events. How can I get started?

Find a nonprofit that is looking for someone to oversee the process. They may have internal staff that can do the behind-the-scenes work, but aren't able to handle the execution to maximize their fund-raising efforts. Present your skills as professionally as possible. List out the things you can do that internal staff cannot. Mention any training, credentials, or certifications specific to event planning that you may have, so the client can see the value of spending on your services to make more in the final analysis.

12

Balancing Your Life

As you make your commitment to your business, you are also investing in yourself. I happen to love what I do, and if you're considering starting your own business you probably do, too. In fact, if you aren't passionate about it, I strongly suggest you reconsider. Owning your own business involves time, hard work, and many difficult choices.

And yet . . . as much passion as you have for your event business, it needs to be balanced with the rest of your life. Creating balance in your life is always a challenge—and if work is your hobby or passion, the lines between what you *want* to do and what you *should* do just seem to become blurrier the busier you get.

To be honest, I don't really think of my business as work. I have so much fun at it that I sometimes have to convince my family I really am working! At the same time, I am perhaps overzealous about creating a professional image for myself and for challenging my colleagues to raise the bar within the industry. I take time to consult with peers, set standards, take a leadership role, meet and formulate long-term goals for the industry, attend and speak at conferences. I spend extra time on the phone, at meetings, and traveling to accomplish these goals. I feel that I have made our industry a better one—but unfortunately, it's often at the expense of my family and friends. They are the ones I leave behind when I go on a business trip, the people I put on hold until I finish my business tasks. This is my own balancing challenge.

You no doubt face challenges of your own in trying to be an event planner, an entrepreneur, a parent, a spouse, a friend, a family member . . . and yourself. Let's take a look at some of these challenges.

Home-Office Guidelines for You, Your Family, and Your Friends

Being in business, especially your own business, requires a full and ongoing commitment. Every day you'll handle inquiry calls, create proposals, think of ways to get new business, discover ideas for new themes or decor, research vendors or contacts, and consider different ways to evaluate your events. Owning a home-based business, while giving you flexibility and freedom, means you never leave your place of work. It's up to you to close the door and create a separate environment. Owning a home-based business also means that you work whenever you can or want to. Your level of commitment will be driven by the time you can give to your business and whatever else is going on in your life. You choose the balance of business and personal life, and you do the work of maintaining this.

Fitting It All In

The minute the last child is out the door in the morning, I make a mad dash to my computer. Then I'm operating in full business gear, checking e-mails, typing proposals, sending memos, planning my daily call list, and following up on prospects. On any given day the race could be interrupted by runs to the bank, to the post office, or even to answer a stray non-work-related phone call. To fit your new home business into your plans, you must take a long hard look at what your day and life are made up of.

Hours of Operation

A prime benefit of owning your own business is owning your own time. Running a business from your home gives you the flexibility to create your own schedule, take lunch when you want to (or not take lunch, which often happens!), and do your errands or family activities when they need to be done.

For your own sanity and to operate at your peak, however, set limits. Mapping out your schedule allows you to plan for the time you spend on your work, for the time you devote to friends and family, and for the time you take for yourself.

Family

It can be difficult to make the transition from work time to family time when your office is in

Extended-Family Time

"Family time" can include parent or sibling time (or aunt, or uncle, or cousin . . .). When I'm traveling on business, I try to plan visits to relatives in the area, giving me an unexpected chance to catch up with a brother or sister-in-law or see how much a niece or nephew has grown. My travel obligations have also given my mother and mother-in-law a chance to spend more time with my children; they often share baby-sitting duties when trips take me away for more than a day or so.

A Day in the Life of an Event Planner

5:30 A.M.	Alarm goes off. Dress and head out for a forty-five-minute walk with the dogs, husband, or friends.
6:30 A.M.	Return home, make coffee, prepare lunches for the kids, make sure everyone's up and moving. Scan the paper. Throw in the laundry.
7:15 A.M.	Wake up third child, Paige, move laundry through, tackle a few household chores.
8:15 A.M.	The house is empty of family. Check e-mails, check daily calendar, plan day accordingly.
9:00–11:00 A.M.	*Scenario One:* Plan for 1:00 P.M. appointment. Finish proposal, print map, assemble sales kit, copy CD demo. Respond to online requests for information, send out memo regarding committee work. Shower, change, be ready to leave at noon.
	Scenario Two: No appointments scheduled. Spend the morning responding to e-mails, finishing necessary memos for committee work, making follow-up phone calls to vendors regarding pricing and other details for upcoming events.
Noon–3:00 P.M.	*Scenario One:* Travel to appointment. Make presentation.
	Scenario Two: Make new-business sales calls. Log into database or file for follow-up.
3:00–5:00 P.M.	*Scenario One:* Stop at vendors for update on new linens. Return to home office, touch base with family, answer messages and e-mails.
	Scenario Two: Work on final touches for upcoming event. Develop final timeline and vendor payment list. E-mail to clients. Discuss changes and make updates. Check on orders for weekend event.
5:00–7:00 P.M.	Family time: Take hockey players to practice. Bring laptop and update projects. Write follow-up thank you notes to clients. Watch part of practice.
7:30–8:30 P.M.	Dinner.
8:30–9:30 P.M.	Household chores. Family time.
9:30–bedtime	Check and answer e-mails. Put final touches on any outstanding projects.

your home. Having a home office lets you slip in some work between dinner and bedtime or between after-school activities and dinner preparations. But it also means that to your family, you're always working! My youngest child occasionally puts her foot down and demands that we do something alone together. A trip to the mall or the movies—or better yet a bike ride or walk in the park—will usually ground us again. Multitasking is a necessity for a busy person, so combining activities can give you some quality time *and* let you get in some exercise.

Although I am often faulted for having the "zone" look on my face when one of my children comes into my office after school to ask a question, I usually am available for rides, sick days, appointments, or sporting practices when needed. I do remind them that I'm working when I am in my office, but they don't always see me as "unavailable" when I'm sitting in the next room at my computer.

To address your family's need for quality time, setting a day or time that you will go over issues or sit and talk may be the best way to go. Being available at a set time and on a regular basis to give your undivided attention will keep the frustration level down on both your part and your family's. The unique balance you create between career and personal time will work if you communicate your needs and expectations and are willing to listen to how everything's working for others. Flexibility and compromise will allow you to "do it all"—or at least do as much as you can to feel good about who you are and what you do!

Friends

My friends know what I do during my day. Occasionally a dear friend will timidly knock on the door to announce that she was passing by and thought she'd stop by for a quick "catch-up." While I seldom take a lunch hour, I welcome an occasional unexpected break in the day to get rejuvenated! I let friends know, though, that if I don't answer my door, it's because I'm on a call and can't be interrupted.

Colleagues

Owning your own business means you are decision maker, idea creator, and chief cook and bottle washer. It's not easy. My advice: Create a network of professionals you can bounce ideas off and get advice from to build a strong business. Find other small-business owners who might share your frustrations or challenges and seek advice on what has worked for them.

Many of my friends are artists and designers, who give me so much inspiration. Others are nurses and caregivers, who create a refreshing counterpoint to the crazed pace that I keep. All of them are important to me, and I constantly remind myself to take time to respect our friendship and give back to them what they give to me.

Caring for Your Children While You Work

If you have or plan to have children, child care is an important consideration. You are committing to a professional image by starting your business, and the fact that it is in your home will not matter to your clients if you start and maintain strict guidelines.

Full Time or Part Time?

When you're just starting out, you may not need full-time care for your children. Still, if you're aggressive with your selling skills and committed to your business, understand that your clients will often demand your full attention. Thus, you must be prepared to cover the child care bases at a moment's notice. You can certainly aim to schedule appointments at convenient times; just remember that meetings often run late, and unexpected events can take you away from your family at any time. Put contingency plans into place just in case you need them.

In-Home Child Care

If you chose in-home child care, make sure your caregivers know that you must not be interrupted when you're in your office. Here's where having a separate area for your office is essential—and preferably *not* right next to the nursery or playroom! Give care providers all the tools they need to care for your child from the moment they arrive straight on through lunch, nap time, and playtime. Set up your daily schedule so they can move from activity to activity without depending on you for information or approvals. And confirm a start and end time to each day so that everyone can plan their schedule accordingly.

What It Costs

Child Care: In-home $10 to $20 per hour (based on level of other assistance they provide, such as transportation, food prep, or light housekeeping when children are napping). Off-site child care $50 to $250 per week (based on time and number of children attending).

Janitorial Services: $8.00 to $15.00 per hour/per cleaner

Bookkeeping/Office Support: $8.00 to $15.00 per hour

Stylist/Personal Shopper: $75 to $125 per hour based on a four-hour minimum

Organizational Consultant: $50+ for telephone or in-home consultations

Spiritual Advisor: $0 to $250+ per hour

Contribution at Local House of Worship: $0 to $20+ per week

Nanny

A live-in nanny is a great way to handle child care if you need suppport outside a typical nine-to-five day. Should your event scheduling demand overnight or weekend child care, a live-in can offer the flexibility you're looking for. Au pairs can offer your family multicultural exposure as well. Be sure to specify your requirements for transportation and scheduling as you screen potential nannies, including details such as getting the children to and from activities after school or on weekends. There are many reliable sources for hiring au pairs. Check in local parenting newspapers or the yellow pages, or ask colleagues and friends for referrals.

Support from Family/Spouse

Child care support from a relative or your spouse can be a wonderful solution and opportunity for everyone. It can offer a bonding experience to both kids and caregivers, and you can concentrate on your work knowing your children are in good hands. Would your children's grandparents, aunts or uncles, or other relatives be available for such an arrangement? Consider compensating the caregivers, and be fair about the time and energy they'll invest. Remember what it takes to chase after a two-year-old. Keeping expectations reasonable will create a positive experience for all parties.

Developing Guidelines

Just as you would with a vendor or client, create a daily schedule for child care professionals. Let them know what is expected of them and the children. Give them the tools to do a great job so you won't be disturbed when you're working. If you're traveling, be sure to provide your caregivers with all pertinent contact information, medical information, and contingency plans in case of emergency. Give them a list of their responsibilities and even reward them for going above and beyond the call of duty. They may be willing to assist outside child care duties if you ask them to and pay them for it. Shopping, laundry, and cook-

Choices, Choices

I often forgo leisure activities to finish a proposal or clean up the details of a project. These are the choices I make. On the other hand I do allow myself to take daily walks. Yes, they're in the wee hours of the morning, but nonetheless I make sure to fit them in. I try to stay up-to-date on current events by skimming the daily newspaper, but I don't often have time for television. I don't go to lunch with friends, but I do meet clients for lunch or dinner. I love to entertain, and many times invite close industry colleagues or even clients to join me for cocktail or dinner parties. These are choices I've learned to make to create a balance I enjoy.

ing can be wonderful bonuses—as long as they don't interfere with the attention your children receive, of course.

Priorities

On any given day, we have commitments. They drive our decisions on how we spend our time. In the best-case scenario, we split our time and energy among several choice areas that we enjoy. More typically, there are the things we have to do, want to do, and wish we could do. Finding the right mix for these items is the test for any well-balanced individual. Throw in the prospect of starting your own business, and you already know what will happen . . . a business takes time, time, and more time. With a generous amount of passion and a large quantity of energy!

Daily Schedule

What does a "typical" day look like for you? Set this down in writing. (No, there are no typical days as an event planner; you'll just have to do your best!) This is the time to simply record your priorities and how you spend your time. Remember to account for the basics—sleeping, eating, and caring for your basic needs. And don't forget driving time as well as routine activities like caring for your home, running errands, and grocery shopping. Make sure you consider the things most important to you and that you *actually* do.

Typically my daily list includes work (meetings, current projects, proposals, and marketing calls), self-care (a daily walk), family time (including my husband), and caring for my home (cooking, cleaning, laundry).

Now expand your scope. What items do you add to your schedule on a weekly basis? For me, these include professional meetings, larger-scale household and yard chores, and church and volunteer obligations. Add your items to your list.

Step back even further and look at your monthly schedule. My own monthly list incorporates visiting family, a book group with friends, entertaining and dining out, and catching a concert or show. You may find that all the really fun things in your life get pushed to your monthly list—it happens all too easily. Whatever *fun* means to you, remember to make time for it.

Now for the hard part: Let's take a look at how the way you actually spend your time compares to your ideal.

Commitments

Make up a list of your own priorities and personal commitments. Be honest about how much time actually devote to each item, and how much you wish you devoted to it. Everyone's list is different, and there are no right or wrong answers here. Besides starting your home-based business, your list could include self-care, family, spouse, home, spiritual needs, friends, exercise, and any number of leisure activities, including reading, bike riding, watching television, travel, and volunteering.

Take a look at how you can organize your time to accomplish more of the goals you set—if not all of them. In any given week you may decide that your business schedule needs to include time for office work, new-business calls and appointments, current project planning and preparations, information gathering and education, and networking. Set up your calendar for each day with these activities scheduled in. Start with deadlines and work backward, adding in a time buffer to ease your stress. If you have to borrow some family time one week to meet a business deadline, pay it back the next week by spending a spontaneous hour with loved ones. They will appreciate being kept on your priority list!

Be realistic about how your business goals fit with your other personal commitments. This will determine what you will get done and when. You may ultimately decide to focus your time on meeting a proposal deadline and attending a special event course, leaving you with only a few

Typical Day Timeline

Time	Self	Family	Work	Volunteerism
Midnight	Sleep			
1:00 A.M.	Sleep			
2:00 A.M.	Sleep			
3:00 A.M.	Sleep			
4:00 A.M.	Sleep			
5:00 A.M.	Exercise with friend			
6:00 A.M.	Self-care			
7:00 A.M.		Organize for day and prepare meals		
8:00 A.M.	Chores	Household chores		
9:00 A.M.			Office	
10:00 A.M.			Appointments	
11:00 A.M.			Calls	
Noon	Eat (quickly!)		E-mails, calls, memos	
1:00 P.M.			Appointments	
2:00 P.M.			Proposals	
3:00 P.M.		Give rides	Calls	
4:00 P.M.		Grocery shop/errands		
5:00 P.M.		Doctor appointments		
6:00 P.M.				Choir rehearsal
7:00 P.M.	Dinner	Dinner		
8:00 P.M.		Chores, family time		
9:00 P.M.			Office work	
10:00 P.M.			Office work	
11:00 P.M.	Bedtime			

Items	Current %	Optimal %	Path to Success
Self			
Family			
Work			
Volunteerism			

hours a week to develop new business and network. You'll also find that your schedule rarely fits into the traditional nine-to-five parameters. That's the beauty of a home office. Don't be afraid to stretch the limits of a "typical" day to allow yourself to accomplish your goals each week.

In a perfect world you could create this list of life values and incorporate each of them into each day—maybe with a different mix of time and priority, but you'd make sure to touch base with them every day.... In the real world, though,

you'll probably want to aim at balancing it on a weekly basis.

Still, here's something to think about: By not putting a bar up, you never raise it. If your priorities and where you actually spend your time don't line up, then it may be time to make a plan for change and put it into action!

Balancing Your Wheel
Home

There's an old saying: None of us ever leaves this world wishing our house was cleaner. Everyone

The Balancing Act

Effective scheduling requires you to weigh your priorities against your deadlines. Scan through the must-do, should-do, and want-to-do lists. What are their various time requirements? How can they be balanced reasonably? If a particular task on my own lists has to be completed by a firm deadline, it moves up in priority so I can make it happen. If I find that my lists are over-crowded or that I'm not accomplishing what I need to, I limit the time I spend on some things. Volunteerism is a big part in my life, for instance—but if I can't find time for my business or family, I need to start limiting my volunteer work.

has a different level of tolerance when it comes to living space. How clean, furnished, and organized your home is really depends on your own style and personality.

The organizational piece of the equation is probably the most important. I find that organization is the key to keeping my stress level down. If things are a mess around me, it's hard to concentrate and comfortably go about my day. For this reason I handle a flurry of household tasks at the very beginning of the day . . . but then I step away from it. Once a week the house gets a top-to-bottom cleaning. Even though I tend to be a creative collector—adding lots of seasonal decor to my tables, walls, and doorways—I also try to be as streamlined as possible to help keep things tidy looking. My two suggestions for keeping your home and your office pleasant: Streamline and organize.

Health

It's true what they say: If you have your health, you have everything. Stress, poor eating habits, and a lack of exercise can all slow you down and keep you from operating at your best. The hour you take from your workday to exercise will renew you and help you to process your tasks more efficiently. The event industry is a creative business. Ideas and fresh thoughts flow from nature, people around us, things we experience and do. By stepping away from your desk to go for a walk or run, you participate in a mini retreat. Enjoy the world around you and mull over your challenges and problems as you take that hour or even half-hour break. You'll be refreshed and approach your "to-do" list with a new perspective.

Self-Care

Just as exercise can offer you a chance to step outside your stress zone, other self-care activities can be critical in helping you operate at an optimal level. Getting in touch with your inner self through meditation, worship, or other introspective practices can help clear your mind and wash away negative and ineffective thoughts and influences. Keep an eye on the positive around you. Look at that half-full glass—and consider the option of no glass! Taking the time to focus on what you need for your soul is as important as meeting your physical needs. The food of life comes in many forms, so treat yourself to a full menu for a strong mind and body.

Outsourcing Your Life

You've learned to outsource your event planning duties . . . now think about whether some parts of your life can be sourced out. My dad once wondered why I insisted on getting to the dump each weekend. I'd encourage my husband to put it on the top of his list for Saturday and stress over it right up until the moment I saw the car leave the driveway with our trash barrels. Of course, this was not my husband's favorite thing to do after a week of work. So my wise father asked me how much trash pickup might cost. I found out it was $10 per week. Was it worth $10 per week to cross this constant worry off two "to-do" lists? Absolutely! I also realized how much time it took me to grocery shop each week. At the time, a delivery service was available that included online ordering and weekly delivery of a full array of groceries: meats, produce, and packaged items. I used that service for several years and cried the day they discontinued it.

Support

My home-based business was born at the same time as my first child. Running a business from my home gave me flexibility and freedom, while still offering challenge and stimulation. The first year I produced one event. The second year I handled two.

Year after year, my business grew. When my children were very young, I had my family care for them when I traveled. Or I took them with me. One trip to San Francisco included my mother and seven-month-old daughter, whom I was not ready to wean at the time. It worked perfectly. I transitioned from pre-event meetings to morning feeding . . . from event setup to afternoon feeding. My mom had a great time, and my little one didn't skip a beat! It was a great memory for my mother and me, and we still look at the photos of Paige riding in the back of a limo in style at the age of seven months!

As my children grew older, they became more independent and realized that even if I might leave for a few days, I would always return. They didn't love the travel, but they loved the goodies they got when I walked back through the door. Now all three children have started to work with me at events. They have seen what it takes to succeed in business from the beginning. My husband has helped me through the downtimes with encouragement, and through the busy times with support that allowed me to travel and give each event my all.

Being in a supportive relationship can make or break your business. No matter how much confidence you may have, hearing about your abilities from someone you love can help you keep your chin up when the going gets tough. And honest

Self-Support

Remind yourself from time to time of everything you've accomplished. It'll help you get through those times when you feel like you're going nowhere fast.

advice when things aren't quite at their best is better received from a loved one than an angry client. If you don't have a partner, your family or friends can offer this support. Share your dreams, ask for assistance—and it will come. But be kind and good to these important people, and take time to let them know you care for them just as much as they care for you.

Frequently Asked Questions

I am having a hard time separating my work from my family responsibilities. How can I make better choices in dividing my time between the two?

Starting your own business is a total commitment, but given the other elements of your life, you will need to create a balance everyone can live with. Maybe you can walk away from the phone after 6:00 P.M., or step away from the computer from 6:00 to 9:00 P.M. and come back to it after the dishes are done and the kids are in bed. Consider how much additional money you will make from the efforts you are putting into your business and the extra time you are taking from your family or personal commitments.

Is it worth getting a sitter for my children when I am working from the home?

If you do not have a spouse who can pick up the slack or an older child to keep an eye out for the little ones, it's worth the peace of mind to get a paid professional to help with child care. Even a student who is willing to act as a mother's helper will allow you to take uninterrupted time for your business. Know your caregiver's limits and your children's needs to make sure they are in good hands and it's not an overwhelming task for the student-helper. It will also help create a more professional appearance when you talk on the phone with clients.

I feel like my business could really take off, if I didn't have any other responsibilities in my life. How can I make my dream come true?

Pace yourself. Make a list. Develop a plan of attack. Check off your successes and feel good about the steps you take. It's easy to look at folks that are wildly successful and say, why not me? The deal is, they may have a bevy of assistants, no other responsibilities other than their business, no family, spouse, or significant other to share their lives with. So in the scheme of things, the baby steps you take can be more impressive in the big picture than you think.

My business is taking up all my time. I've given up my gym membership, quit my Bunco group, and stay in to work most evenings. Do you think I am on course for success?

It depends how you define success. Many ideas come from giving yourself time to think, be creative, and get ideas and input from others. Walking the dog can combine exercise with pet care and—if you join a friend—with companionship. It can also give you a chance to throw creative ideas out and get feedback. Don't feel that you can live in a vacuum or that you are cutting your business time short by taking a break. Let your mind relax, and it just may be the break needed to let the next good idea take root. Joining clubs or volunteer groups can also be a good source of networking and new business. Balancing your wheel will help your business run smoothly!

13

Being the Best: Education and Training

The fact that you are interested in starting your own event planning business shows you have the desire to work in the field of special events. But do you have the necessary skills to start and grow a home-based event planning company? The event process is full of challenges, as you've seen throughout this book. With the right tools and training, though, all these challenges can be met with safe and creative solutions. You have many options for formal training to help you build your skills for a rewarding and exciting career in special events.

Formal Education

In chapter 1, I talked about the basic skills you'll need to run your business. While it may not be necessary to get an MBA, it's not a bad idea to take business courses. They will certainly help you run your business in a professional way and will save you time and money in the long run. The focus of your training, though, should be in the area of special events.

Currently degree programs in special events are offered both throughout the United States and internationally. These four-year programs will give you a wide-ranging foundation of knowledge to begin your career in event planning. If you aren't in a position to study full time, distance learning classes and part-time programs may allow you to work and study at the same time.

Even after completion of a degree program, be prepared to allow yourself time to gain the very necessary experience that school training just can't provide. You'll certainly understand the process of developing

Being the Best

Education:

- Formal education
- Monthly professional meetings
- Semiannual or annual professional conferences

Experience:

- Networking with colleagues
- Apprenticeship with experienced planners
- Critical evaluation procedures

A combination of a good formal foundation in events and business, monthly professional meetings that offer strong educational content and the chance to network with colleagues, yearly conferences, and critical evaluation of your planning procedures will help you continue to offer the very best in planning services.

visit from the fire chief might shut down your event while the guests are arriving. If you don't know the importance of involving the venue's engineering department when you're using fog machines, you may end up with the fire alarms blaring and the hotel evacuated an hour after the event begins. These are just a few of the ways that events can end in disaster. Training and experience will help you fully prepare for each event.

Professional Designations

There are many designations available in the hospitality industry, all designed to guarantee your qualifications in various key areas.

The Certified Special Events Professional (CSEP) designation is the premier certification if you want to truly stand out in the special events industry. The requirements for the CSEP title combine basic knowledge of the event planning process with experience. This is a great natural stepping-stone if you've completed classroom training, have worked for a few years, and want to elevate your professional credentials.

This designation is offered by the International Special Events Society (ISES). Enrollment information can be found on the Web at www .ises.com. The process involves filling out an application that includes a point sheet calculating attendance and leadership in ISES, education, experience, industry and community service, publications, and awards. Once approved, you begin preparation for an exam on core competencies in event management, dictionary terms, and a case study essay. You are also required to submit professional recommendations.

an event with your degree in hand but not the unexpected curveballs that the job will throw you. Even with meticulous contingency planning, you'll find yourself challenged to solve problems at almost every event.

My recommendation is to balance ongoing formal education with apprenticeships and strong mentors. Formal training will at least give you exposure to the event preparation process. The danger, however, is that you won't realize everything you *don't* know. If you don't stay up to date on risk procedures, for instance, you may not realize how dangerous some event situations can be. If you don't understand permitting, a surprise

Professional Designations in the Special Event and Related Industries

Special events:

- Certified Special Events Professional (CSEP): www.ises.com
- Professional Bridal Consultant (PBC): www.bridalassn.com
- Accredited Bridal Consultant (ABC): www.bridalassn.com

Meetings:

- Certified Meeting Professional (CMP): www.conventionindustry.org
- Global Certification in Meeting Management (CMM): www.mpiweb.org
- Certified Association Sales Executive (CASE): www.pcma.org
- Certified Association Executive (CAE): www.asaenet.org
- Certified Planner of Professional Meetings (CPPM), Certified Internet Meeting Professional (CIMP), Certified Global Meeting Professional (CGMP): www.cimpa.org
- Learning Environment Specialist (LES): www.pcma.org

Destination management:

- Destination Management Certified Professional (DMCP): www.adme.org
- Certified Destination Management Executive (CDME): www.iacvb.org

Hospitality:

- Certified Hospitality Account Executive (CHAE): www.hftp.org
- Certified Hospitality Marketing Executive (CHME): www.hsmai.org
- Certified Hospitality Technology Professional (CHTP): www.hftp.org
- Certified Hospitality Sales Professional (CHSP), Certified Food and Beverage Executive (CFBE), Certified Hotel Administrator (CHA), Certified Lodging Manager (CLM), Certified Hospitality Supervisor (CHS), Master Hotel Supplier (MHS), Certified Hospitality Trainer (CHT), Certified Hospitality Educator (CHE): www.ei-ahla.org

Travel:

- Certified Incentive Travel Executive (CITE): www.site-intl.org
- Certified Corporate Travel Executive (CCTE): www.nbta.org

Exhibition:

- Certified in Exhibition Management (CEM): www.iaee.org
- Certified Manager of Exhibits (CME): www.tsea.org
- Certified Trade Show Marketer (CTSM): www.exhibitornet.com

Venues:

- Certified Facilities Executive (CFE): www.iaam.org
- Certified Hospitality Marketing Executive (CHME): www.hsmai.org

Food:

- Certified Professional Catering Executive (CPCE): www.nace.net
- Foodservice Management Professional (FMP): www.nraef.org
- Certified Culinary Professional (CCP): www.iacp.com

Achieving certification or striving for a professional designation shows your ability to combine basic knowledge with implementation. It indicates your commitment to professionalism in the industry. It also will set you apart from your competitors who aren't certified.

If you plan to focus on the wedding industry, a Professional Bridal Consultant designation would be an excellent goal. If you want to focus on partnering with the meeting and convention industry, the Global Certification in Meeting Management or a Certified Meeting Professional designation may be a good choice. There are many other designations within the hospitality industry focusing on disciplines such as catering, exhibit and display, and travel. See page 161 for an overview of issuing organizations and their Web sites. You can also turn to appendices A and B for more information.

More Ways to Refine Your Trade
On-the-Job Training

While formal training provides a sound start for your business, on-the-job training will complement your strategy and provide the much-needed experience to turn you into a "think-on-your-feet" professional. Rather than experience the event process on paper alone, plan to put your learning to use. You might begin by working on projects with other experienced planners or volunteering for a community event. Be critical of your skills, and you'll know when the time is right to start out on your own.

Continuing Education Programs

If you're already working in the industry and want to round out your skills, check local listings for community college, university, or high school continuing education courses. Offerings can include courses in basic business skills, events skills, nonprofit planning, catering, floral design, use of costuming or theatrical components in events, entertainment, public speaking, and marketing.

These courses can be relatively inexpensive, are usually offered at convenient times and locations, and can provide an excellent base on which to build your business.

Industry Conferences and Courses

To really get an educational shot in the arm, commit to attend an event industry conference. These conferences are great ways to receive training, network with fellow event professionals, and stay on top of current trends. They allow you to gather resources and ideas on how others execute the event process.

The International Special Events Society traditionally holds a three-day conference each August called Eventworld. The days are jam-packed with sessions on an array of event topics; evenings typically showcase the host city's best venues decorated in contemporary and unique themes created by local event professionals. The ISES Esprit Award Dinner is held on the final evening, with the prestigious industry awards being given to winners throughout the world. These conferences also provide ample time to network with fellow planners and chat about the event industry. The educational sessions also include CSEP prep courses to help candidates prepare for certification. Attendance at these conferences will help you accrue points for certification as well. Information can be found on the ISES Web site at www.ises.com.

The Special Event (TSE), held each January, delivers a similar experience. This conference has an additional trade show feature, with exhibitors showcasing products and services specifically used in the event industry. It's a great way to pick up new ideas and products to add to your events. Daily educational sessions, evening parties, and a closing gala celebration with an award dinner are also offered. The event is produced by Primedia Business Exhibitions; for more details, check out www.thespecialeventshow.com.

Event Solutions Expo (www.event-solutions.com) is held during late summer and offers a similar conference experience combining education and a trade show. Additional conferences include the CSEME Conference and Expo (February) in Toronto and the Canadian Special Events Expo (March) in Vancouver. Information on these can be found at www.canadianspecialevents.com. See appendix B for a listing of professional organizations and associated conferences and expos.

Regional Education Conferences

Another option for conference attendance that may be closer to home are the regional education conferences offered by ISES. These are held throughout the world and are organized by the ISES regions (Northeast, Southeast, West, Midwest, Asia Pacific, and EurAfrica). These are a scaled-down version of Eventworld, with a similar combination of education, evening activities, and networking. There are sometimes award presentations and exhibitor showcases as well. These are often an accessible way to gain information, enjoy valuable educational sessions, and network with colleagues without breaking your travel budget.

Trade Shows

Trade shows can help you update your supplier lists—and can provide networking opportunities as well. Many of the industry Web sites will offer information on shows that focus on event-related products and services. BiZBash (held each October; see www.bizbash.com) is specifically designed for the special event industry. Others, such as the Stationery Show, focus on a narrow aspect of the business but can provide excellent up-to-date resource information. Keep an eye on professional publications or do a thorough online search to find exhibitions or shows in your area.

Mentors

If you look through your resource directory or card file, I'm sure you'll find a list of colleagues whom you regard as professionals in the industry. They can be an excellent source of advice and training as you start and grow your business. As long as you aren't perceived as direct competition, many planners are flattered by an interest in their business practices and will welcome the opportunity to coach you. You will also see how others handle business duties such as billing, training employees, and event execution.

Another great place to find mentors is at your local ISES meetings. Most seasoned professionals are happy to help someone avoid the pitfalls they weathered, while sharing the lessons they learned along the way.

Don't discount the importance of a business-focused mentor to support your growth in running a home-based business. I have received invaluable advice from other successful home-based entrepreneurs on how to balance home and work, how to find good temporary help, and how to manage my business like a pro.

Apprenticeships

Before you begin the time-consuming and emotionally intense process of starting a business, consider serving time as an apprentice. There may be a seasoned planner out there who's looking for someone to handle day-to-day tasks and would be willing to train you and bring you up through the ranks. A retirement-age planner with no plan for passing the business to a family member might be willing to sell you his or her business when the time is right.

Above and Beyond

As you develop your business and planning skills and gather a strong portfolio of projects, you may reach a point where your home-office setting just isn't working for you. You have outgrown the two file cabinets you proudly purchased when your business was a fledgling. You walk into your home and see evidence of your business in every room and on every surface. Perhaps you cannot park your car in your garage or have run out of storage space for those unique "must-have" decorations that you've come to realize you'll use infrequently. It's time to think about the next step.

Expanding

If you truly like your home-office setup, consider staying where you are and expanding. Depending on your real estate market and your own personal situation, home expansion may allow you to create an office above a garage, or build another wing onto your home that can be later used as an in-law apartment or au pair suite. For some planners a small home-based business gives them the flexibility they want with the option for added income. It can be the perfect balance between family and work, without having to commit to climbing a corporate ladder. Only you know if your business is where you want it to be, or you're craving for more.

Partnering

Perhaps joining forces with another planner may be attractive to you. Before you reach the breaking point, begin to examine the work style, ethics, and personalities of planners you may consider partnering with. They may have an office outside the home that would provide the necessary space for your blossoming business. You may find that your portfolio will complement theirs to provide an even wider array of services to clients.

With partnering comes consideration of the legal implications. Check with your attorney for issues relating to partnerships and ownership of your business. If you are both home-based and are leaving your homes to begin this new larger business, you'll be on an even playing field and have fewer issues with ownership fairness.

Adding Staff

When your business is at the point that you just can't do it all yourself—and your work is generating profit—it may be time to make the commitment to hiring employees. Depending on your home, this may necessitate a move to a larger space to provide a professional and productive environment for work. It would be wise to consider a storage area at this point as well to take back the personal space you've given up over the years with your event props and decor.

Hiring formal employees brings with it an array of legal and personnel issues. Consult with your attorney to find out the full ramifications of this move to make sure it's right for you.

What Else Is Out There?

You will reach a point in your business when you consider retirement or moving on to another venture. What kind of plan can you put into place for passing down or selling your business? If you've managed your finances well and show strong profits, you may have created an entity that is viable and attractive for purchase. Perhaps you've nurtured a strong assistant who has proven him- or herself and is interested in taking over the business. At the start of your business, these issues seem inconsequential, but as time goes on they become real decisions for you to ponder.

As you've worked through the exciting and challenging aspects of building your special event planning business, you may have discovered other areas that interest you. You may be intrigued to expand your offerings as you uncover skills and interests you didn't realize you had. You may see a niche market or unique aspect of the business that you want to explore. Don't be afraid to follow your heart, your talents, and current trends and market conditions to enable yourself to continue making money and enjoying what you do. There are no top secrets to running a successful business; it's simply a matter of passion for what you do, the ability to look at yourself critically, and the urge to be the best you can be. Take it one step at a time, and be proud that you create such pleasure for others by your excellence in planning special events!

United States—Four-Year Programs

- Appalachian State University *(NC)*—Meeting & Convention Management, Destination Management.

- Arizona State University.

- Florida International University—Culinary Event Management; Travel Information Technology; Planning Meetings and Conventions; Meetings and Show Markets; Exposition and Events Management; Catering Management; Advanced Events Management.

- George Washington University *(DC)*—Event Management Certificate Program: Best Practices in Event Management; Event Coordination; Event Marketing; Risk Management: Legal and Ethical Safeguards; Corporate Event Management; Meetings and Conferences; Sport Event Marketing and Management; Starting, Growing and Managing an Event Business; Event Sponsorship; Government Event Strategies; Catering Design and Coordination; Exposition/Trade Show Planning, Management, and Marketing; Wedding Planning, Coordination, and Consulting Workshop; Celebrating Historical Events; Event Fundraising; Introduction to Event Information Systems (EIS); Event Laboratory; Protocol for Event Managers; Event Entertainment and Production; Green Meetings and Events; Destination Management Companies; Event Fundraising and Sponsorship. Master's Concentration in Event Management (Master of Tourism Administration—MTA): Event Management; Conference and Expositions Management; Directed Research; 9 tourism courses—36 credits total. Accelerated Master's of Tourism Administration with a Concentration in Event Management.

- Georgia State University *(Atlanta)* School of Hospitality Administration—6 courses: Meeting and Trade Show Management; Trade Show Management; Meeting Planning; Convention Service Management; Corporate Sponsorship; Facility Usage.

- Indiana University/Purdue University at Indianapolis—2 courses: Introduction to Convention and Meetings Management; Meeting and Convention Sales.

- Kansas State University—Convention Service and Meeting Planning.

- Keuka College *(NY)*—Meeting and Convention Planning.

- Mercyhurst College *(PA)* Hotel, Restaurant—4 courses: Principles of Meetings and Conventions Management; Convention and Trade Show Management; Catering Management and Operations; Promotional Strategies for Meetings and Conventions.

- Metropolitan State College *(Denver, CO)*— 5 courses: Principles of Meeting and Travel Administration; Meeting Administration I (Convention Management); Tour Planning; Meeting Administration II (Special Events Management); Catering and Menu Planning.

- New Mexico State University *(Las Cruces)*— Bachelor of Science in Hotel, Restaurant, and Tourism Management.

- New York University—Hotel, Restaurant, and Food Management; Music and Entertainment Management for Meeting Planners; Music Marketing.

- Niagara University *(NY)*—4 courses: Tour Planning, Design, and Packaging; Attractions and Event Management; Meeting and Convention Services; International Destination and Convention Management.

- Northeastern State University *(OK)*—Bachelor of Business Administration in the Meetings and Destination Management School (accredited by the Accreditation Commission for Programs in Hospitality Administration and approved by the Professional Convention Management Association).

- Purdue University *(IN)* Restaurant, Hotel, Institutional, and Tourism—Associate and Bachelor of Science degrees from the Hospitality and Tourism Management Department of the College of Consumer and Family Sciences.

- Robert Morris College *(PA),* Dennis Rudd— Catering and Events Marketing.

- Roosevelt University *(Chicago, IL)* Manfred Steinfeld School of Hospitality and Tourism Management—2 bachelor's degrees with majors in Hospitality Management and Tourism and emphasis in Meeting Planning; 1 certificate program in Meeting Management consisting of 5 undergraduate courses: Introduction to Meeting Planning, Convention and Exposition Management; Applications and Techniques of Meeting and Conference Management; Issues and Trends in Meeting and Conference Management; Special Events; and Exposition Management; also 1 graduate course, Graduate Seminar in Meeting and Conference Management, as an elective for the Master's of Science in Hospitality and Tourism Management (MSHTM).

- San Jose State University Hospitality Management—Conference, Convention, Meeting Planning; Event Planning.

- Southern Illinois University at Carbondale—1 special studies course on topics in meeting planning.

- University of Central Florida, Rosen College of Hospitality Management—Bachelor of Science in Hospitality Management, Event Management, and Restaurant and Food Service Management; Masters in Hospitality and Tourism Management; PhD in Hospitality Education.

- University of Houston Hilton College of Hotel Administration—Convention and Meeting Management; Catering; Event and Public Facilities Management; Current Issues in Convention Services.

- University of Massachusetts at Amherst, Hotel, Restaurant, and Tourism—Meeting Planning.

- University of Nevada, Las Vegas, Tourism and Convention Department, Harrah College of Hotel Administration—Undergraduate courses include Introduction to the Convention Industry; Meeting Planning; Convention Sales and Service; Trade Show Operations; Exposition Service Contracting; Special Events Management; Exhibit Marketing and Management; Association Management; Catering Operations and Sales; Destination Marketing (CVB Management); Convention Facility Management; Sport and Concert Arena Management; Destination Management (DMC Management); Festival and Events (a hands-on capstone course); Incentive Travel; International Exposition Management; Meetings and Event Coordination; Internship. Distance learning: Executive Master's Program in Meetings, Events, Conventions, and Events (MECE). Undergraduate classes online.

- University of New Hampshire, Whittemore School of Business Economics—BS in Hospitality Management.

- University of New Orleans, Kabakoff School of

Hotel, Restaurant and Tourism Administration— 4 courses: Introduction to the Conventions, Events, and Meetings Industry; Meeting, Event, and Convention Planning; The Management and Planning of Conventions, Events, and Meetings; Convention Destination Management.

- University of South Carolina—Conference and Meeting Planning; Catering Management.

- University of Southern Mississippi—Hotel and Restaurant Management; Convention & Meetings Management.

- Virginia Polytechnic Institute and State University—Hotel, Restaurant, and Institutional Management; Intro Meetings and Convention Management; Catering Management.

- Washington State University.

New England Schools for Higher Education in the Meeting, Event, and Hospitality Industry

Northeastern University

360 Huntington Avenue
269 Ryder Hall
Boston, MA 02115
Phone: (617) 373–2400; (617) 373–2419; (617) 373–7972
www.ace.neu.edu

Northeastern University offers the Meeting and Event Planning Program. Courses in this program emphasize practical knowledge and are beneficial to those new to the profession as well as veterans in the field. Courses are taught by industry professionals with extensive firsthand event and meeting planning experience.

To earn a Professional Meeting and Event Planning Certificate, participants must successfully complete six of the following seven courses:

- Introduction to Meeting Management
- Program Design
- Budgeting, Financial Management, and Negotiation Techniques
- Site Selection
- On-Site Conference Management
- Audio-Visual Technology
- Contract Management

The university offers a winter and spring schedule at its downtown Boston and Dedham, Massachusetts, campuses.

Johnson & Wales University

8 Abbott Park Place
Providence, RI 02903
Phone: (800) DIAL–JWU; (800) 342–5598; (401) 598–1000
The Hospitality College: main (401) 598–1476; dean (401) 598–4764
www.johnsonandwales.com

Johnson & Wales is a highly respected university whose students are focused on a career education in business, hospitality, culinary arts, or technology. Majors and degree programs are offered at the undergraduate, graduate, and doctoral level.

Johnson & Wales has campuses located in Providence, Rhode Island; North Miami, Florida; Denver, Colorado; and Charlotte, North Carolina. In addition, J&W students have the opportunity for international study at the Göteborg, Sweden, campus.

Programs are available in Hospitality; Food Service Management; International Travel and Tourism Studies; Sports, Recreation, and Event Management; Hotels; Culinary Arts; Baking and Pastry Arts; and Culinary Nutrition.

Boston University

School of Hospitality Administration
www.bu.edu/hospitality/
Dean James Stamas
928 Commonwealth Avenue
Boston, MA 02215
Phone: (617) 353–3261
Fax: (617) 353–6328
busha@bu.edu

This program prepares students for management positions in the hospitality industry. Along with hospitality courses, students take a variety of liberal arts and management courses to develop a well-rounded education, focusing on the skills they need to succeed in the business world.

The university also offers a certificate program in the culinary arts. This program exposes students to the best professional chefs and teachers in the cooking world at a first-rate training facility. Students are trained in the basic classical and modern techniques, introduced to theories of food production, taught how to become creative chefs, and introduced to other professions in the food industry.

The program's stated goals are:

- To expose dedicated culinary students of all ages to the best professional chefs and teachers in the world of cooking.

- To train students in the basic classic and modern techniques and theories of food production.
- To introduce students to the various disciplines of gastronomy.
- To introduce students to various cultures and cuisines.
- To teach future chefs how to become creative chefs.

University of New Hampshire (UNH)

15 College Road, McConnell Hall
Durham, NH 03824
Raymond Goodman Jr., PhD, Chair of Hospitality Management Department
Phone: (603) 862–3303
www.unh.edu
www.wsbe.unh.edu/Dept_HospMgmnt/index.cfm

The University of New Hampshire's program in Hospitality Management is one of only five programs worldwide that is accredited by both the American Assembly of Colleges and Schools of Business (AACSB) and the Accreditation Commission for Programs in Hospitality Administration (ACPHA). The primary emphasis of the program is on the hospitality industry, but graduates are prepared for management roles in all areas of the service sector.

Graduates have gone on to positions in lodging and food service, retirement facilities, software companies, the tourism, travel, and recreation fields, and institutions such as hospitals, nursing homes, colleges, and schools.

Bay State College

Boston Campus
Day and Continuing Education/Evening Programs
122 Commonwealth Avenue
Boston, MA 02116
www.baystate.edu
Phone: (617) 236–8000; (800) 81–LEARN (53276)
Fax: (617) 536–1735

Gloucester Campus
Continuing Education/Evening Programs
Gloucester High School
32 Leslie O'Johnson Road
Gloucester, MA 01930
Phone: (617) 217–9800 or (617) 217–9801
Fax: (978) 282–4809

Middleborough Campus
Continuing Education/Evening Programs
Middleborough High School
71 East Grove Street
Middleborough, MA 02346
Phone: (617) 217–9829
Fax: (508) 946–8281
Admissions office: admissions@baystate.edu

Middlesex Community College

Bedford and Lowell, Massachusetts, campuses
Middlesex@middlesex.mass.edu
Phone: (800) 818–3434
Out of state: (978) 656–3370

Middlesex Community College is nationally accredited by the Association of Collegiate Business Schools and

Programs (ACBSP) for the offering of its business programs culminating in the Associate in Science in Business Administration degree. The Hospitality Management program is designed to prepare students for entry-level positions, management training programs, or career advancement in hotel and restaurant management. Students are required to earn sixty-three credits.

Certificate in Hospitality Management programs are designed for individuals who need to acquire specific job skills in a short period of time in order to advance or expand employment and career opportunities. Courses taken in certificate programs may also be directly applied to related Associate in Science degree programs. The Hospitality Management certificate provides the basic skills needed for employment in the hotel and restaurant management fields. Students are required to earn twenty-four credits.

The Certificate in Travel Services Management programs are also designed for individuals who need to acquire specific job skills in a short period of time in order to advance or expand employment and career opportunities. The Travel Services Management certificate provides the basic skills needed for employment in the travel services industry. Students are required to earn twenty-four credits.

North Shore Community College

1 Ferncroft Road
Danvers, MA 01923
Phone: (978) 762–4000
www.northshore.edu/

The Tourism and Hospitality program provides students with the knowledge and skills needed for entry-level positions in a variety of tourism and guest services industries. Upon completion of this program, students will be prepared for entry-level employment in hotel/resort/lodging establishments, tourist attractions, museums, meeting planning, convention/conference centers, visitor bureaus/chambers of commerce, and tour guide services. Also offered is a Tourism/Hospitality Internship and the Tourism/Hospitality Cooperative Education program.

The program is also beneficial to individuals currently working in the tourism and hospitality industry who may wish to enhance their knowledge and skills and/or earn a degree by enrolling in some or all of the courses in the program.

United States—Two-Year Programs

- Austin Community College *(TX)*—Meeting and Event Planning Certificate and Associate's Degree in Hospitality Management with a specialization in Meeting and Event Planning. Department of Hospitality Management courses include: Convention and Group Management and Services; Special Events Design; Introduction to Convention/Meeting Management; Applied Convention/Meeting Management; International Convention/Meeting Management; Exposition and Trade Show Operations; Destination Management; Advanced Topics in Tourism; Travel Industry Management; Special Topics in Travel & Tourism; Destination Specialization.

- Chemeketa Community College *(OR)*—Travel and Tourism Industry; Catering and Banquet

Operations; Special Events Planning; Meeting and Convention Management.

- Cloud County Community College *(KS)*.

- El Paso Community College *(TX)*—Convention and Meeting Planning.

- Madison Area Technical College *(WI)*—Meeting and Event Management Degree: Fundamentals of Meeting Management; Meetings Industry Budgeting and Financial Management; Incentive and Special Events Management; Meeting Coordination; Exposition Management; Risk Management, Negotiations, and Legal Issues; Tourism Management; Meeting and Event Internship. Contact Janet Sperstad (608–246–6372).

- Mount Hood Community College *(OR)*—Conventions and Meeting Management; Special Events and Attractions Management; Catering, Restaurant and Food Management: Concept to Customers; Introduction to Travel and Tourism.

- Northern Virginia Community College—6 courses: Introduction to Meeting Planning; Introduction to Association Management; Principles of Meeting Planning; Exhibition and Exposition Management; Meeting and Exposition Law and Ethics; Meeting and Exhibition Marketing; Internship in Meeting Planning.

- Richland College *(Dallas, TX)* offers an AAS degree in Travel, Exposition, and Meeting Management, and a certificate in Travel and Tourism. Contact M. T. Hickman, Program Coordinator. Courses: Introduction to

Convention/Meeting Management; Introduction to Travel and Tourism; Exposition and Trade Show Management; Convention and Exposition Law and Ethics; Hospitality and Special Events; Applied Convention/Meetings Management; International Meeting Management.

- Skyline College *(CA)*—5 courses: Introduction to Meeting Management; Principles of Meeting Management; Principles of Meeting and Convention Management; International Expositions; International Business Protocol; Special Events Management.

Australia

- La Trobe University, School of Sport, Tourism and Hospitality Management, offers a Bachelor of Business degree in Tourism and Hospitality Management as well as a Master of Business degree (research) and a PhD. Courses: Special Event and Meeting Industry Management; Special Events, Conferences, and Meetings; Banquet and Convention Catering Management.

Canada

- Atlantic Tourism and Hospitality Institute *(Charlottetown, PEI)*—Events and Convention Management. Contact Maureen Webster.

- Ryerson University, School of Hospitality and Tourism Management *(ONT)*—Event Management Certificate Program: 11 courses: Best Practices in Event Management; Catering Design and Coordination; Corporate Event Management; Event Coordination; Event Fundraising;

Event Marketing; Meetings and Conferences; Risk Management: Financial, Legal, and Ethical Safeguards; Starting, Growing, and Managing an Event Business; Protocol for the Events Manager; Wedding Planning, Coordination, and Consulting Workshop.

- Thompson Rivers University *(BC)*—Events and Convention Management Diploma. Contact Ted Wyckes.
- University of Calgary—Tourism and Hospitality Management.

Great Britain

- Leeds Metropolitan University, School of Tourism and Hospitality Management, UK Centre for Events Management—BA (Hons) Events Management, HND Events Management.

Korea

- Hallym University *(Seoul)*—Master's degree program. Contact Dr. Ginny Suh.

Alliance of Meeting Management Companies (AMMC)

7465 Prairie Lake Drive
Indianapolis, IN 46256
Phone: (317) 842–9852
Fax: (317) 576–9851
www.ammc.org

AMMC, founded in 1997, strives to be the premier organization for meeting management consultants; serve the business management needs of meeting management consultants; establish an identity for the meeting management consultant industry, both in the meetings industry (planners and suppliers) and in the general business community; create a network that supports the members; encourage and promote high standards and ethics in the meetings industry; and safeguard and promote the interests of its members.

AMC Institute (Formerly IAAMC)

100 North Twentieth Street, fourth floor
Philadelphia, PA 19103
Phone: (215) 564–3484, ext. 2220
Fax: (215) 963–9784
www.amcinstitute.org

AMC Institute is an international nonprofit trade association comprised of companies that provide association management and professional services to volunteer-governed organizations and for-profit companies. AMC Institute includes member companies that are demonstrated leaders in the association industry, committed to high quality and value-added association management and professional services.

American Hotel & Lodging Association (AH&LA)

1201 New York Avenue NW
Suite 600
Washington, DC 20005
Phone: (202) 289–3100
Fax: (202) 289–3199
www.ahla.com

The American Hotel & Lodging Association (AH&LA), founded in 1910 with 11,400 hotel members, represents the interests of the U.S. lodging industry at the national level on federal legislative and regulatory affairs, the national media, the educational community, research groups, and the general public.

American Society for Training and Development

Membership Department

P.O. Box 1567

Merrifield, VA 22116-1567

Phone: (703) 683–8100; (800) 628–2783

Fax: (703) 683–1523

www.astd.org

The American Society for Training and Development (ASTD) is the world's largest association dedicated to workplace learning and performance professionals. ASTD's members come from more than one hundred countries and connect locally in 140 U.S. chapters and twenty-four global networks. Members work in thousands of organizations of all sizes, in government, as independent consultants, and suppliers. ASTD started in 1944 when the organization held its first annual conference. ASTD has widened the profession's focus to link learning and performance to individual and organizational results and is a sought-after voice on critical public policy issues.

American Society of Association Executives (ASAE) & The Center for Association Leadership

1575 I Street NW

Washington, DC 20005

Phone: (202) 626–2723

Fax: (202) 371–0870

www.asaenet.org

The American Society of Association Executives (ASAE), founded in 1920 with 24,940 members, is dedicated to enhancing the professionalism and competency of association executives, promoting excellence in association management, and increasing the effectiveness of associations to better serve their clients.

Association for Convention Operations Management (ACOM)

191 Clarksville Road

Princeton Junction, NJ 08550

Phone: (609) 799–4900

Fax: (609) 799–7032

www.acomonline.org

The Association for Convention Operations Management (ACOM), founded in 1988 with 400 members, is an international organization for convention professionals. The association is dedicated to providing needs-directed continuing education, enhancing professional values and standards, and advancing and promoting quality customer services, to encourage growth and recognition of the convention services profession.

Association of Collegiate Conference and Events Directors–International (ACCED-I)

Colorado State University

8037 Campus Delivery

Fort Collins, CO 80523

Phone: (970) 491–5151

Fax: (970) 491–0667

www.acced-i.org

Founded in 1980, the Association of Collegiate Conference and Events Directors–International (ACCED-I) is a nonprofit organization committed solely to the collegiate conference and events profession. Its mission is to improve, promote, and recognize excellence in the collegiate conference and events industry. Celebrating more than twenty-five years of service, ACCED-I is the premier resource for collegiate-based conference and event planners. Currently, ACCED-I has a membership of more than 1,500 professionals representing approximately 640 educational institutions and forty-one corporations in the United States, Canada, and the United Kingdom.

Association of Destination Management Executives (ADME)

3401 Quebec Street
Suite 4050
Denver, CO 80207
Phone: (303) 394–3905
Fax: (303) 394–3450
www.adme.org

The mission of ADME is to increase the professionalism and effectiveness of destination management through education, promotion of ethical practices, and availability of information to the meeting, convention, and incentive travel industry and the general public.

Center for Exhibition Industry Research (CEIR)

2340 Trinity Mills Road
Suite 107
Carrollton, TX 75006
Phone: (469) 574–0686
Fax: (469) 574–0699
www.ceir.org

CEIR is a nonprofit organization with the mission of advancing the growth, awareness, and value of exhibitions and other face-to-face marketing events by producing and delivering research-based knowledge tools. For more than twenty-five years, CEIR has been highlighting the importance of exhibitions in today's business environment.

Connected International Meeting Professionals Association (CIMPA)

9200 Bayard Place
Fairfax, VA 22032
Phone: (512) 684–0889
Fax: (267) 390–5193
www.meetings2go.com

Founded in 1982, CIMPA is an online association of buyers and sellers of meeting and travel products and services with a mission. The mission of CIMPA is to connect people of different cultures through meetings, travel, and the Internet for the purpose of promoting understanding, tolerance, and friendships. By being connected to each other and to resources on the Internet, members of this community will more easily share tools, information, and ideas to plan cost-effective and successful meetings, travel, and incentives. With more than 3,000 members in thirty-two countries on five continents, CIMPA's members collectively plan more than 100,000 meetings annually. Its annual International Technology, Meetings and Incentives Conference is held in different locations all over the world.

Convention Industry Council (CIC)

1620 I Street NW, sixth floor
Washington, DC 20006
Phone: (202) 429–8634
Fax: (202) 463–8498
www.conventionindustry.org

The Convention Industry Council's thirty-two member organizations represent more than 103,500 individuals, as well as 17,300 firms and properties involved in the meetings, conventions, and exhibitions industries.

Formed in 1949 to provide a forum for member organizations seeking to enhance the industry, the CIC facilitates the exchange of information, develops programs to promote professionalism within the industry, and educates the public on its profound economic impact. In addition to the CMP Program, CIC is also responsible for the Hall of Leaders Program as well as the Accepted Practices Exchange (APEX).

Council of Engineering and Scientific Society Executives (CESSE)

P.O. Box 130656
St. Paul, MN 55113
Phone: (952) 838–3268
www.cesse.org

The Council of Engineering and Scientific Society Executives (CESSE) was organized some years ago as an informal meeting of the principal executive officers of the societies to provide a forum for mutual exchange of experience and guidance, and discussion of common problems in operating the societies. The objective is to advance the arts and sciences of the management of engineering and scientific societies.

Destination Marketing Association International (DMAI)

2025 M Street NW
Suite 500
Washington, DC 20036
Phone: (202) 296–7888
Fax: (202) 296–7889
www.destinationmarketing.org

Destination Marketing Association International represents 1,350-plus professional members from more than 600 destination marketing organizations throughout thirty countries. Called the International Association of Convention & Visitor Bureaus until August 2005, the association has worked to enhance the professionalism, effectiveness, and image of CVBs and tourism boards since 1914.

Exhibit Designers & Producers Association (EDPA)

5775 Peachtree-Dunwoody Road
Suite 500-G
Atlanta, GA 30342
Phone: (404) 303–7310
Fax: (404) 252–0774
www.edpa.com

Exhibit Designers & Producers Association (EDPA) members include exhibit designers; producers; systems manufacturers; distributors and marketers of custom, portable, and modular exhibits; show services contractors; exhibit transportation companies; event marketers; and organizations that provide related products or services to the exhibit industry. EDPA provides members with industry-specific education, advocacy, research, and marketing networking opportunities.

Exhibition Services & Contractors Association (ESCA)

2260 Corporate Circle
Suite 400
Henderson, NV 89074
Phone: (702) 319–9561; (877) 792–ESCA (3722)
Fax: (702) 450–7732
www.esca.org

Exhibition Services & Contractors Association (ESCA) is the professional organization of firms engaged in the provision of material and/or services for trade shows, conventions, exhibitions, and sales meetings. ESCA is the voice of the exhibition service industry, and its purpose is to be a source of facts and answers to special problems that confront the convention service industry.

Financial and Insurance Conference Planners (FICP)
401 North Michigan Avenue, twenty-second floor
Chicago, IL 60611
Phone: (312) 245–1023
Fax: (312) 321–5150
www.ficpnet.com

Financial and Insurance Conference Planners (FICP) is an association whose membership is comprised of meeting, convention, and conference planning professionals who work for or are under contract to insurance or financial services companies. Members exchange meeting management techniques and ideas that enhance the value of conferences and promote the professional stature and career growth of planners.

Healthcare Convention & Exhibitors Association (HCEA)
5775 Peachtree-Dunwoody Road
Suite 500-G
Atlanta, GA 30342
Phone: (404) 252–3663
Fax: (404) 252–0774
www.hcea.org

The Healthcare Convention & Exhibitors Association (HCEA) is a trade association of more than 670 organizations united by their common desire to increase

the effectiveness and efficiency of health care conventions and exhibitions as an educational and marketing medium. HCEA promotes the value of exhibits as an integral part of health care meetings. HCEA offers its members a continuing opportunity to become more knowledgeable in their profession through meaningful communication, the exchange of ideas with other members, and the many services provided exclusively to HCEA members.

Hospitality Financial and Technology Professionals (HFTP)
11709 Boulder Lane
Suite 110
Austin, TX 78726-1832
Phone: (512) 249–5333; (800) 646–4387
Fax: (512) 249–1533
www.hftp.org

Hospitality Financial and Technology Professionals is an international professional association. Formed in 1952, HFTP now has more than 4,600 members around the world.

Hospitality Sales & Marketing Association International (HSMAI)
8201 Greensboro Drive
Suite 300
McLean, VA 22102
Phone: (703) 610–9024
Fax: (703) 610–9005
www.hsmai.org

The Hospitality Sales & Marketing Association International (HSMAI) represents travel sales and marketing professionals. Founded in 1927, HSMAI is an international individual membership organization comprised of more than 5,000 members representing seventy-nine chapters in thirty-five countries worldwide, dedicated to enhancing sales and marketing management skills in the travel and hospitality industry through education and networking opportunities with peers and customers.

International Association for Exhibition & Events (IAEE) (formerly IAEM)

8111 LBJ Freeway
Suite 750
Dallas, TX 75251
Phone: (972) 458–8002
Fax: (972) 458–8119
www.iaem.org

The International Association for Exhibition & Events (IAEE) is the professional association for more than 3,200 individuals located in forty-one nations, and it is involved in the management and support of the global exhibition industry. IAEE's mission is to promote the exhibition industry throughout the world and to provide for the education and professional growth of its members.

International Association of Assembly Managers (IAAM)

635 Fritz Drive
Suite 100
Coppell, TX 75019
Phone: (972) 255–8020
Fax: (214) 255–9582
www.iaam.org

The objectives of the International Association of Assembly Managers (IAAM) are to promote and develop professional management of public assembly facilities; to foster use of these facilities for the benefit, recreation, and entertainment of the public; to cultivate acquaintance and communication among managers of such facilities; to circulate information of value to the members and the public so as to develop more frequent and efficient use of such facilities; to standardize practices and ethics of management and relationships with the public; to develop and maintain liaisons with national and international organizations in allied fields; and to provide other related services that promote the advancement of the association.

International Association of Conference Centers (IACC)

243 North Lindbergh Boulevard
Suite 315
St. Louis, MO 63141
Phone: (314) 993–8575
Fax: (314) 993–8919
www.iacconline.com

The International Association of Conference Centers (IACC) is a not-for-profit organization founded in 1981 to advance understanding and awareness of conference centers as distinct and unique within the hospitality industry.

International Association of Culinary Professionals (IACP)

304 West Liberty Street
Suite 201
Louisville, KY 40202
Phone: (502) 581–9786
Fax: (502) 589–3602
www.iacp.com

IACP is a not-for-profit professional association that provides continuing education and development for its members, who are engaged in the areas of culinary education, communication, or in the preparation of food and drink. The worldwide membership of nearly 4,000 encompasses more than thirty-five countries. This diversity not only offers unique insight into the world's cuisines but provides excellent networking opportunities. IACP's vision is to be an international forum for the development and exchange of information, knowledge, and inspiration within the professional food community worldwide.

International Association of Protocol Consultants Ltd. (IAPC)

P.O. Box 6150
McLean, VA 22106
Phone: (703) 759–IAPC (4272)
Fax: (703) 759–4277
www.protocolconsultants.org

The mission of the International Association of Protocol Consultants (IAPC) is to advance the practice of protocol, etiquette, and civility worldwide by providing members with higher learning opportunities, promoting ethical and professional standards, facilitating exchange of information, and encouraging an inclusive community for all professionals. Membership consists of experienced producers and/or directors of events involving world leaders, heads of state, foreign dignitaries, and corporate executives. Members include special event planners, meeting professionals, corporate/international executives, protocol consultants, diplomatic/government protocol officers, etiquette teachers, medical professionals, attorneys/legal counselors, and entrepreneurs.

International Association of Speakers Bureaus (IASB)

7150 Winton Drive
Suite 300
Indianapolis, IN 46268
Phone: (317) 328–7790
Fax: (317) 280–8527
www.iasbweb.org

IASB member bureaus subscribe to a code of professional conduct and accepted practices. Being in direct contact with an IASB member bureau assures the meeting professional of securing the right speaker and/or trainer for their event. In many cases, IASB speakers' bureaus hold the key to a successful event.

International Congress and Convention Association (ICCA)

Entrada 121, NL-1096 EB
Amsterdam
The Netherlands
Phone: 31–20–398–1919
Fax: 31–20–699–0781
www.iccaworld.com

With more than 600 member organizations and companies in eighty countries, ICCA provides a worldwide network of meeting professionals, experts in all aspects of hosting and organizing congresses and conventions. ICCA offers its members unique opportunities to access comprehensive meetings data, exchange business leads, and meet potential clients. ICCA represents all the various professional meeting suppliers, such as congress travel and destination management companies; airlines; professional congress, convention, and/or exhibition organizers; tourist and convention bureaus; meeting information and technical specialists; ICCA meetings hotels; and convention and exhibition centers.

International Special Events Society (ISES)

401 North Michigan Avenue
Chicago, IL 60611
Phone: (312) 321–6853
Fax: (312) 673–6953
www.ises.com

The mission of ISES is to educate, advance, and promote the special events industry and its network of professionals along with related industries. To that end, it strives to uphold the integrity of the special events profession, acquire and disseminate useful business information, foster a spirit of cooperation among its members and other special events professionals, and cultivate high standards of business practices.

Meeting Professionals International (MPI)

3030 LBJ Freeway
Suite 1700
Dallas, TX 75234
Phone: (972) 702–3000
Fax: (972) 702–3070
www.mpiweb.org

Established in 1972, MPI is the largest association for the meeting profession, with more than 20,000 members in sixty-eight chapters and clubs across the United States, Canada, Europe, and other countries. As the global authority and resource for the $122.3 billion dollar meetings and events industry, MPI empowers meeting professionals to increase their strategic value through education, clearly defined career pathways,

and business growth opportunities. MPI launched Pathways to Excellence in 2003, which has taken meetings to the next level of inclusion in the business world.

National Association of Catering Executives (NACE)

9881 Broken Land Parkway
Suite 101
Columbia, MD 21046
Phone: (410) 290–5410
Fax: (410) 290–5460
www.nace.net

The National Association of Catering Executives (NACE), founded in 1958, is the oldest and largest professional association for caterers in all disciplines and their affiliate vendors. With more than 3,000 members in forty-six chapters, NACE serves hotels, off-premise, club, military, and on-premise caterers, providing top-quality educational and networking opportunities and affiliate vendor interaction.

National Business Travel Association (NBTA)

110 North Royal Street, fourth floor
Alexandria, VA 22314
Phone: (703) 684–0836
Fax: (703) 684–0263
www.nbta.org

The National Business Travel Association (NBTA) is the source for critical information on the business travel industry. For more than thirty-five years, NBTA has dedicated itself to the professional development of its members through advocacy, education and training, and networking opportunities. NBTA represents more than 2,500 corporate travel managers and travel service providers, who collectively manage and direct more than $170 billion of expenditures within the business travel industry.

National Coalition of Black Meeting Planners (NCBMP)

8630 Fenton Street
Suite 126
Silver Spring, MD 20910
Phone: (202) 628–3952
Fax: (301) 588–0011
www.ncbmp.com

The National Coalition of Black Meeting Planners (NCBMP), founded in 1983, is a nonprofit organization dedicated primarily to the training needs of African-American meeting planners. It is the purpose of NCBMP to be the preeminent organization in education of the African-American meeting planner in all aspects of the meeting planning profession.

National Speakers Association (NSA)

1500 South Priest Drive
Tempe, AZ 85281
Phone: (480) 968–2552
Fax: (480) 968–0911
www.nsaspeaker.org

The National Speakers Association (NSA) is an international association of more than 3,800 members dedicated to advancing the art and value of experts who speak professionally. For more than twenty-five years, NSA has provided resources and education designed to enhance the business acumen and platform performance of professional speakers.

Professional Convention Management Association (PCMA)

2301 South Lake Shore Drive
Suite 1001
Chicago, IL 60616
Phone: (312) 423–7262
Fax: (312) 423–7222
www.pcma.org

The mission of the Professional Convention Management Association (PCMA) is to serve the association community by enhancing the effectiveness of meetings, conventions, and exhibitions through member and industry education and to promote the value of the meetings industry to the general public.

Religious Conference Management Association (RCMA)

1 RCA Dome
Suite 120
Indianapolis, IN 46225
Phone: (317) 632–1888
Fax: (317) 632–7909
www.rcmaweb.org

The Religious Conference Management Association (RCMA) is a professional nonprofit interfaith organization of men and women who have responsibility for planning and/or managing meetings, conferences, conventions, or assemblies for religious organizations. Founded in 1972, RCMA is dedicated to enhancing the professionalism of its members and to improving the experience of religious meeting attendees throughout the world.

Society of Government Meeting Professionals (SGMP)

908 King Street
Lower Level
Alexandria, VA 22314
Phone: (703) 549–0892
Fax: (703) 549–0708
www.sgmp.org

The Society of Government Meeting Professionals (SGMP) is dedicated to improving the knowledge and expertise of individuals in planning and execution of government meetings through education, training, and industry relationships.

Society of Incentive & Travel Executives (SITE)

401 North Michigan Avenue
Chicago, IL 60611
Phone: (312) 673–4902
www.site-intl.org

The Society of Incentive & Travel Executives (SITE) is a worldwide organization of business professionals dedicated to the increased recognition and use of incentives as a motivator and reward in programs designed to achieve defined objectives. Founded in 1973, SITE is comprised of 2,000 individual members representing more than eighty countries.

Trade Show Exhibitors Association (TSEA)

McCormick Place
2301 South Lake Shore Drive
Suite 1005
Chicago, IL 60616
Phone: (312) 842–TSEA (8732)
Fax: (312) 842–8744
www.tsea.org

The Trade Show Exhibitors Association (TSEA) provides knowledge to management professionals who utilize the trade show and events medium to promote and sell their products, as well as those who supply them with products and services. Since 1966, TSEA has been distributing thoughtful publications and meaningful services that help exhibitors do their jobs more effectively.

Business Books

Applegate, Jane. *201 Great Ideas for Your Small Business*. Princeton: Bloomberg Press, 1998.

Jones, Laurie Beth. *Jesus, CEO*. New York: Hyperion, 1995.

Kantor, Rosabeth Moss. *World Class: Thriving Locally in the Global Economy*. New York: Touchstone, 1995.

Parinello, Anthony. *Selling to Vito*. Holbrook, Mass.: Adams Media Corporation, 1999.

Pine, B. Joseph II, and James H. Gilmore. *The Experience Economy*. Boston: Harvard Business School Press, 1999.

Williams, Terrie. *The Personal Touch*. New York: Warner Books, 1994.

Creativity Boosters

Magazines: *Architectural Digest, Martha Stewart Living, Town & Country, House & Garden, House Beautiful, Garden Design, Veranda, Elle Décor, Metropolitan Home*

Event Basics

Goldblatt, Joe, CSEP. *Special Events: The Best Practices in Modern Event Management*. 3rd ed. New York: John Wiley & Sons, 2002.

Goldblatt, Joe, CSEP, and Kathleen S. Nelson, CSEP. *The International Dictionary of Event Management*. 2d ed. New York: John Wiley & Sons, 2001.

Hemela, Deborah Ann. *The Sourcebook: Props, Set Dressing & Wardrobe*. Altadena, Calif.: Debbies Book, 2002–2003.

Nonprofit Risk Management Center. *Managing Special Event Risks*. Washington, D.C.: Nonprofit's Insurance Alliance of California, 1997.

Professional Convention Management Association. *Professional Meeting Management*. Birmingham: Professional Convention Management Association, 1996.

Tutera, David, and Laura Morton. *A Passion for Parties*. New York: Simon & Schuster, 2001.

Wiersma, Elizabeth A., CSEP, and Kari E. Strolberg. *Exceptional Events: Concept to Completion*. Weimar, Tex.: Chips Books, 2003.

Home Office

Morgenstern, Julie. *Organizing from the Inside Out*. New York: Henry Holt & Company, 1998.

———. *Time Management from the Inside Out*. New York: Henry Holt & Company, 2000.

Life Balance

Ford, Debbie. *The Dark Side of the Light*. New York: Riverhead Books, 1998.

McGraw, Philip. *Self Matters: Creating Your Life from the Inside Out*. New York: Free Press, 2001.

Richardson, Cheryl. *Life Makeovers*. New York: Broadway Books, 2000.

———. *Stand Up for Your Life*. New York: Free Press, 2002.

———. *Take Time for Your Life*. New York: Broadway Books, 1998.

Networking

Carnegie, Dale. *How to Win Friends and Influence People*. New York: Simon & Schuster, 1982.

Darling, Diane. *The Networking Survival Guide*. New York: McGraw-Hill, 2003.

Bar and Bat Mitzvahs

www.mitzvahplan.com/handbook.html

www.bnaimitzvahguide.com

www.barbatmitzvahguide.com

www.birthdayexpress.com/bexpress/planning/
BarMitzvah.asp

Budgeting/Financial Planning

Microsoft

www.microsoft.com/smallbusiness/resources/
startups/budgeting.mspx?xid=OVPI524

Home Business Magazine

www.homebusinessmag.com

About

http://financialplan.about.com/msubbudg.htm

Expense Watch

www.expensewatch.com

U.S. Small Business Association

www.sba.gov/library/pubs/fm-8.pdf

Business Week Online

www.businessweek.com/smallbiz

American Express

www10.americanexpress.com/sif/cda/page/
0,1641,638,00.asp

Business Planning

U.S. Small Business Administration

www.sba.gov/smallbusinessplanner/plan/index.html

SCORE

www.score.org

American Express Small Business

www133.americanexpress.com/osbn/Tool/biz_plan

Business Plan Archive

www.businessplanarchive.org

PricewaterhouseCoopers

www.pwcglobal.com

Small Business Info Canada

http://sbinfocanada.about.com/od/businessplans

So You Wanna.Com

www.soyouwanna.com/site/syws/bizplan/bizplan
.html

Entrepreneur Magazine Online
www.entrepreneur.com/businessplan/index.html

Microsoft Small Business Center
www.microsoft.com/smallbusiness/resourots/
startups/business-plans.mspx

Intuit/Quicken
www.quicken.com/small_business/run

Small Business/About
http://sbinformation.about.com/od/businessplans

Event Planning Tools

Planning Events.com: Internet source for planning
tools and ideas
www.planningevents.com/Articles.php

Meetings Industry Megasite: Tools, resources, articles,
and news
www.mimegasite.com/mimegasite/index.jsp

Events Planning Tools
www.planenstyle.com

Catering Resources

Caterease/Horizon Business Services
www.caterease.com

CaterMate
www.catermate.com

CaterPro
www.caterprosoftware.com

Caterware
www.caterware.com

Culinary Software Services
www.culinarysoftware.com

Synergy International
www.synergy-intl.com

Event Business Management Resources

NetSuite
www.netsuite.com

Intuit—makers of QuickBooks, Quicken
www.quicken.com

ReNTiT
ReServe Interactive/Efficient Frontiers
www.efficient-frontiers.com

TimeSaver Software
www.timesaversoftware.com

Vivien Layout Software
www.viviendesign.com

Rental Resources

Party Track/Event Rental Systems
www.partytrack.com

General Special Events Resources

http://specialevents.com
www.partyspot.com
www.birthdayexpress.com/bexpress
www.orientaltrading.com
www.partyamericastore.com
www.party411.com
www.party.lifetips.com

www.shindigz.com

www.appetizerstogo.com/party_tips.asp

www.evite.com/pages/party/partytips.jsp

www.clubmom.com (click on "Your Life," "Holidays & Parties")

Fund-Raising/Nonprofit

www.nonprofit-connections.org

www.usa.gov/Business/Nonprofit.shtml

http://resources.tnpr.ca

www.not-for-profit.org

www.fundraising.co.uk

www.fundraisingnetwork.org

www.fundraisingdirectory.com/FundResources.htm

Legal/Ethical Issues

ASCAP:

www.ascap.com

BMI:

www.bmi.com

Performing rights organization for songwriters and publishers:

www.SESAC.com

Convention Industry Council:

www.conventionindustry.org

APEX:

www.conventionindustry.org/apex/apex.htm

Marketing

Entrepreneur magazine

www.entrepreneur.com/marketing/index.html

U.S. Small Business Association

www.sba.gov/starting_business/marketing/basics.html

More Business

www.morebusiness.com

Small Business UK

www.smallbusiness.co.uk

About.com

http://marketing.about.com/cs/sbmarketing/l/aa060103a.htm

Microsoft

www.microsoft.com/smallbusiness/resources/articles.mspx

Small Business Canada

http://sbinfocanada.about.com

Business Link

www.businesslink.gov.uk/bdotg/action/home

Meeting/Conference Planning

Star Cite

www.starcite.com

National Internet Resources for Event Planners

www.event-planner.com

Certain Software

www.certain.com

www.mimegasite.com

www.bls.gov/opub/ooq/2005/fall/art03.pdf

Decor

Dream World Backdrops: www.dreamworld
backdrops.com

Registration Systems

www.cvent.com

www.regonline.com

www.sporg.com

www.eRSVP.com

www.kintera.com

www.certain.com

Products/Vendors

BBJ Linen
www.bbjlinen.com

Cloth Connection
www.clothconnection.com

Discount Candles
www.discountcandleshop.com

NJ Candle Company
www.njcandle.com

Oriental Trading Company
www.orientaltrading.com

Rentals Unlimited
www.rentals-unlimited.net

Sensia Candles
www.sensia.com

Table Fashions
www.tablefashions.com

Table Toppings
www.tabletoppings.com

Table Toppers
www.tabletoppersinc.com

Wedding Resources

www.fulfilledatlast.com

www.weddingsolutions.com

www.brides.com

www.knotforlife.com

www.theknot.com

www.yourwedding101.com/

Work/Life Balance

http://management.about.com/od/lifeworkbalance

www.business.com/directory/human_resources/
work_and_life

http://stats.bls.gov

www.lime.com/balance

Balance and Spirituality

www.brigidsplace.org/journal/Keeping-a-Spiritual-
Balance-in-a-Busy-Life.asp

Organization

www.homeofficelife.com/ask_expert.html

www.queenofclutter.com

www.organizingresources.com/1index2.htm

Stress Management

http://stress.about.com/About_Stress_
   Management.htm

www.stressbusting.co.uk

Time Management Tips

www.timemanagementgoals.com/freetips.htm

www.ineedmoretime.com/time_tips.htm

www.thrivewithadd.com/thrive/pdf/time_sense_
   exercise_tool.pdf

Index

About the Author

Jill S. Moran, CSEP, began her career in special event planning in 1990 by planning a client reception for 500 guests attending an international trade show. Drawing on her background in the arts, exhibit and display experience, and an instinct for creativity and planning, her event portfolio now includes such clients as Philips Netherlands, Nokia, Duracell, the Dannemiller Educational Foundation, and Schwarzkopf Technologies.

Jill has grown her award-winning company, jsmoran, special event planning & management, from trade show events to providing creative advice and full-scale implementation and production of special events ranging from corporate outings and sales and marketing events to nonprofit conferences, fund-raising galas, and exclusive parties. She has hosted events in cities across the country and internationally, in locations ranging from museums and yachts to convention centers and wineries. Her events have been televised on *Entertainment Tonight* and E!. She has been showcased on Boston's Channel 7 WHDH-TV sharing design and party decorating ideas.

She has served on several international committees for ISES, the International Special Events Society, and has been president of the New England Chapter. She was one of the first designated Certified Special Events Professionals in the New England area and was a 2003 winner of the prestigious ESPRIT award for excellence in event production and design. In 2005 she was awarded an ESPRIT for Best Industry Contribution for *How to Start a Home-Based Event Planning Business*. Jill has lectured at The Canadian Special Events & Meeting Expo, Eventworld, The Special Event, and ISES Regional Education Conferences and has participated on panel discussions for industry conferences.

Her varied background includes a degree in music education, MBA coursework, and continued involvement in the arts and education on a community level. She lives in Massachusetts with her family and continues to enjoy creating the life of the party!